1

Super Tough: Mental Strength. Tenacity. Perseverance. Never Give Up.

By Patrick King
Social Interaction Specialist and
Conversation Coach
www.PatrickKingConsulting.com

Table of Contents

Chapter 1. Toughness Determines Your Life

Tough times don't last; tough people do. – Robert Schuller

Mental toughness is to physical as four is to one. – Bobby Knight

Someday Isle. Land of disenchantment. A place populated by unhappy people who are fed up and have a habit of settling. You don't want to end up here.

The inhabitants of Someday Isle—which is actually a huge island that looks much smaller from afar—have neglected to work their way up through hardship. In fact, they've thoughtfully and deliberately avoided it. They've attained few of their dreams and none of the ones that required hard work and perseverance.

It's the mecca for the world's most ungratified people, though it has a pretty nice downtown strolling area.

There's quite a bit of travel to Someday Isle simply because it's so easy to get to. There's even ferry service! When people want to see Someday Isle, they gather on the shores of the mainland and look at it without needing a telescope or binoculars.

Someday Isle welcomes all; it actually sucks people in. Most of them never leave it, even though they have the oars to a rowboat right in front of them.

What is this mysterious force that allows select people to leave Someday Isle? Simple mental toughness.

Let's talk about Susan. She's wanted to be an actor since age eight. As a young girl, she wondered how grownups could possibly get away with playing pretend every day. When she learned that they could not just get away with it but get *paid* for it, she made her first major career decision in third grade.

Once Susan discovered that one could actually *study* acting, she began to understand that it was much more than just playing dress-up on television and pretending to be fabulous ice skaters and ballerinas. But she never tried out for any school plays, thinking she wouldn't be able to hack it. A small but significant voice in her head told her, "That's all right. Someday I'll find a way to make it work."

Still possessing a motivated spirit, Susan went to college as a theater major. But college wasn't like high school. The competition was stronger, and everyone in her program was as passionate as she was. The professors were more intimidating. She tried out for a big part in a small theater production and ended up switching her major to sociology. Still, she thought, "Someday I'll gather the courage. And when I do..."

After college, Susan moved to New York City. She was geared to work harder than anyone else. She even considered stepping far out of her comfort zone and auditioning for an improv comedy group. But she didn't when she saw that they preferred people with experience. She reminded herself of her childhood dream: "Someday I'll have enough experience."

Amidst a multitude of low-paying waitress jobs and a short stint as an auctioneer, Susan began to feel overwhelmed and anxious. It was simply too tough for her. She moved back home and took the first job she could get: working as a data-entry temp in an office. It was a far cry from what she had imagined as a child, but it was comfortable and, above all else, safe.

Aside from that, the only aspect about her new job was that the office had a beautiful ocean view. Some days, Susan would take lunch in the break room overlooking the water. On one of those days she squinted through the window at the ocean and noticed a land mass out in the distance—it was large but gray and rocky and clouds always seemed to be circling it. Susan didn't know it at the time, but she'd been to that island many times—it was Someday Isle.

The Importance of Toughness and Tenacity

You may have figured out by now that Someday Isle is a metaphor stemming from people wistfully lamenting, "Someday I'll get there..." It represents where we end up when we lack the drive, tenacity, or toughness to get to where we *really* want to go. Someday Isle is not a desirable destination, yet it's an incredibly well-populated island.

We keep hope alive by resolving to do something about it in the future—"*Someday I'll* finally get this done." But what happens is we get acclimated to this state of mind—it starts to feel oddly but unhappily comfortable—and as it sets in, we just stay in that mindset and watch our dreams pass us by.

It's sad, because those goals are achievable. Just about all of them. But to overcome those very real, ghastly fears and doubts, at some point, the rubber must meet the road and we need to be jolted into foreign and uncomfortable situations.

Toughness is internal strength. It implies you have a reserve of comfort in handling adverse situations. It means being resolute in your aspirations, not being compromised by environmental changes or unfamiliar circumstances. Toughness makes you always ask, "And so what?" in the face of hardship to focus on moving forward. It simply means you'll find a way.

It's pushing through and blowing past handicaps, not giving up at the first, second, third, or one-hundredth sign of trouble or defeat. It's the will to constantly drive one's self forward until their goal is comprehensively and completely accomplished, not giving up even when they might have a great excuse for doing so.

Tough people are motivated by conquering the challenges they come across—hence the overused but still accurate catchphrase, "When the going gets tough, the tough get going." What sets the top 1% apart from everyone else is how setbacks are dealt with. We can't control everything that happens to us, but we can certainly control how we respond to it.

Toughness is difficult, and for that reason, it is important for self-growth. It requires us to challenge our established ways of dealing with situations and implement massive change. And human beings are resistant to change. Shaking up our personal status quo can be actively uncomfortable; even if our stasis holds us back from opportunities, we stay in that mode because it's easy.

But it's important to remember that being resistant to change is a choice that we make. It's voluntary. It's not something that's forced upon us by our situation, our upbringing, or the things that have happened to us in life. Staying idle is a selection we make—just as much as choosing to build on our toughness and tenacity. We *choose* to accept the comfort of failure and deny the anxiety that comes with the risk necessary to be successful.

Toughness is required for anything big we want to achieve. Being resistant and "safe," on the other hand, is the reason we fail. Someone who's become self-sufficient in business or life hasn't done so because they're more intelligent or naturally talented—there are undoubtedly professors and experts who are smarter and more gifted than they are. In fact, there are *failures* who might be smarter and more gifted than them. But they've managed to succeed because they didn't give up. They saw obstacles in the path to their achievement and systematically powered through them by not resisting change. That's tenacity, and it's as much a factor in personal development as anything you learn in school or on the job.

Being tough and tenacious doesn't mean not feeling fear or anxiety. Plenty of situations cause the tough and tenacious at least incidental worry or nervousness at the outset. It's simply making the choice to deal, confront, fight, and persevere. They handle fear like a certainty of life—they work through it, displace it, and maybe even use it as a motivator.

One of the best illustrations of toughness and tenacity comes from some of the hardest-headed (in a literal manner) athletes on the face of the earth: players in the British Premier League of football ("soccer" to Americans).

Two British universities in Lincoln and Liverpool conducted interviews with coaches for an unnamed British Premier League club. They sought to establish what made Premier players better than others who hadn't advanced to the top tier of British football. The researchers' first assumption was that surely talent was the sole separator between the so-called upper and lower professional ranks. Their conclusions proved them right, as they painted a portrait of tenacity in action.

Coaches said the best players developed mentally tough tendencies at an early age. They showed a lot of personal independence by taking on responsibility for their actions and not being threatened by others. They felt in control of their fates. At the same time, they were very receptive and cooperative with their coaches and instructors since they were always focused on improving their play.

Premier players were found to not be intimidated by challenges—in fact, they welcomed them and saw them as opportunities to prove themselves. They liked the feeling of being dared to overcome obstacles and embraced the chance to do so. They also took a healthy approach to failure: even if they fell short or erred time after time, they saw such experiences as necessary steps to learning. Making mistakes wasn't something they feared; it was expected and natural. Such errors gave them the chance to adjust and adapt their style of play or strategize their efforts around their specific abilities and limitations.

The researchers also found that the football players tended to maintain strong self-discipline away from the field. Many of them had given up the life of the so-called normal teenager, choosing instead to spend hours building their skills and improving their play. Their fortitude at home and in school paved the way for success—on both the football pitch (that's what they call a soccer field) and in their non-playing lives. Their tendencies toward self-directed learning and improvement made them stand out in comparison to their peers.

Lower-level players, on the other hand, required a lot more oversight and outside direction. They depended on the support of others and usually deferred to somebody else when it came time to dealing with issues or solving problems. They were more likely to believe in their own limits and stop pushing in the face of adversity. Despite their skill, their mental components just weren't going to elevate them to the top-tier level.

You may not, in fact, be a professional soccer player. But the study showed how toughness is built through everyday situations in people willing to embrace challenge. Tough people don't shy away or recoil from criticism or adverse circumstances—they expect them and set themselves up to learn from them.

Failure doesn't faze them because they know it's coming, in some form or another. They live by the action-movie maxim, "If it doesn't kill you, it just makes you stronger." And so far, nothing's killed them. Toughness is a trait one simply has to develop if their ambitions are high. It's one of the few common threads among people who get far in life, and it's what will carry you to where you want to go.

Let's circle back to Susan for a minute.

Her ambition was strong, but she didn't have any measure of toughness to overcome her moments of doubt. She balked at the idea of having to work hard for minimal, momentary gain, even if it meant she'd eventually reach her goal. The prospect of putting herself out for judgment and vulnerability filled her with dread, and she was utterly unprepared to fight her way through it for an extended period of time.

Enter Valerie. She took drama in high school and majored in theater in college, just as Susan did. But Valerie spent a lot more time perfecting her craft, past the point where she had as vibrant of a social life as her friends. She auditioned for multiple plays each semester, fine-tuned her skills, and created a long-lasting relationship with failure.

When Valerie got to New York, she faced rejection after rejection for a few months, to the point where she almost expected it. The experience built a "nothing to lose" attitude within her, and Valerie went to auditions with a resolute and determined stance—even if she didn't get a part, she'd keep going for it.

There was no Someday Isle option to act as a way out. She was determined to push through it, withstanding the temporary moments of defeat and boredom she knew would happen. Eventually, Valerie impressed a casting director—not just because she had the talent, but because the director sensed that whatever she needed to get done would get done.

Valerie didn't *deny* the hurt of being rejected—she felt it but didn't let it define her. She was determined to deal with it and move on. That built her up, and over the course of her life, it made her a formidable person. Toughness alone won't make you elite in whatever you want, but without it, you'll have no chance.

Toughness Saboteurs

Developing toughness is a commitment, and to stay on track requires incredible alertness that doesn't come naturally. People aren't born with it—it's an acquired skill that one learns out of necessity. It doesn't suddenly manifest itself in your life; rather, it comes through making the tough and correct decisions time after time on a daily basis. Each fork in the road will either reinforce your mental toughness or tear it down until you're at the point that it's instinctual.

As such, there are many obstacles to toughness, many of which are subconscious patterns of thought. They all serve to allow you to take the easy way out and generally practice *weakness* versus strength.

Author Theodore Bryant outlined some of the ways we are derailed from toughness in his book *Self-Discipline in 10 Days*. Bryant personifies the mentally weak part of us as "Hyde," which is a very appropriate reference to *Dr. Jekyll & Mr. Hyde*, literature's *original* split personality.

It's Hyde who wants us to run free from self-responsibility and indulge in the most hedonistic and instant gratifications—and here are some of the ways he does it. It's worth noting that you may not be engaging in these consciously, and you might even believe yourself when you internally speak them. But try to take a step back and see how familiar you might be with the following disempowering thoughts, and ask if you are being completely honest with yourself.

Cynicism. Whenever we internally debate whether to persevere or not, the weak voice inside us is going to question whether it's going to make any difference or be worthwhile. To that end, it's going to fixate on flaws, breaches, or failures and inflate them: "What's the point of exercising? It doesn't work." "You're never going to have enough time to learn a foreign language and you're probably not going to ever afford to go to a place where you can use it, so why bother?"

Of course, this is a pattern of thought that allows us to take the easy path out. The counterpoint to cynicism is to acknowledge that nothing is ever perfect. There will always be mistakes, flaws, and setbacks on whatever road we are traveling. It may indeed not make a difference or be worthwhile. But you'll never know that beforehand, and all you are doing is not even allowing yourself the opportunity to seek greater.

Negativism. Our inner Hyde will focus on the negative aspects of anything they don't want to do. These are probably extraordinarily small or unimportant details that have zero impact on the big picture. But that doesn't matter—they'll find 'em and talk about them until they're convinced a leg is about to fall off. "Work out? No thank you. Do you *know* how sweaty and gross public gyms are? They're filthy!" "Why do you want to try and open up a restaurant anyway? You'll never have a holiday off of work again!"

The antidote to negativism is much like the one for cynicism: anticipate and expect it. Given enough time and room for rumination, one can find something negative about everything under the sun— even *good* things like celebrations or accomplishments. Most of these negative things are of little or no consequence to anyone but the internal pleasure-seeker who's trying to keep you from working. Place those negative things in context and weigh the minuscule costs that are keeping you away from massive benefits.

Defeatism. This might be the most dangerous of all self-sabotages, as it speaks directly to your own abilities and resources or lack thereof. Defeatism is the belief that *you can't do it*—that you're not capable, intelligent, dexterous, or talented enough, so why bother? "You have always sucked at math, so why do you think you can learn basic accounting for your job?" "You're not smart enough to understand the complexities of running your own business, so why bother?"

So much great potential has been wiped out by the self-fulfilling prophecy of defeatism. The way to combat it is to remind yourself, as often as possible, that you *can*. People with less ability or talent than you have accomplished great things, whereas some of those with *more* are just as prone to struggle as you think *you* are (probably due to their own sense of defeatism). Even if you can't do it right now, you can improve and get better to the point that you can do it. Ability is not a fixed quantity, but by not exercising toughness to push yourself and persevere, you are keeping it fixed.

Escapism. Taking on a new challenge like building toughness always raises one's anxiety level. You're about to embark on a new course, and fear of the unknown almost inevitably kicks in. And when the body experiences anxiety, its fight-or-flight response might lean toward the latter: leave the scene and escape. "Look, I don't know if today's a great day to start a CrossFit program. Don't you have some fantasy football lineups to set?" "Geez, look at all those people at that networking event you want to go to. People are intimidating. Let's take in a movie."

No change, positive or negative, ever happens without a moment of anguish— more than a few, in fact. It's part of the plan. Without that discomfort, true transformation can't really take place. Imagine the pain and anxiety *not* accomplishing your goal will cause, because it will be more profound and deflating than the most acute of growing pains. Just remember that when you feel those pains, the process is working, and the next stage of triumph over them is just around the corner.

Delayism. This is similar to escapism in that it's just a way to avoid making any meaningful progress in developing toughness. But it's nothing more than stalling: a nearly empty moment of inaction in which you just stand around and develop excuses for not starting. "How are you going to write 750 words a day unless you have a plan for what you're going to talk about?"

"You can't start planning this business idea until you have all the right productivity software. Wait until they're on sale."

In anything you're trying to do to better yourself, *some* activity is better than *no* activity. In some cases, it's even *preferable* to start before you're ready so you can learn what to do as you go. Everything you do counts, and even if your situation or resources aren't up to standards yet, you can still make meaningful progress until they are. There is never a perfect time for anything, and no amount of planning will make you fully, 100% prepared. It's a myth that keeps you paralyzed. Nobody ever learned less by taking the long way—so embrace the notion of baby steps or jumping into something before you're 100% prepared.

These acts of self-sabotage happen once in a while, and sometimes they might all fly into your brain simultaneously. Your weak mind, however much we hate Hyde most of the time, is an integral part of keeping you safe and guarded. Sometimes Hyde is even right.

But for our purposes, he is far too overzealous and is keeping you from realizing your potential. Be mindful of these thinking patterns and learn to battle them. Actions start from thoughts.

The Biology of Toughness

To embody toughness, it's also important to understand just how it develops from a biological standpoint. That way, you can set yourself up for success and not act against your own best interests. For the most part, the answer lies in one of the brain's favorite chemicals: dopamine. Dopamine is a neurotransmitter, a chemical that drives response messages to different parts of the brain. Neurotransmitters are associated with different responsibilities depending on the physiological condition they're responsible for—immunity, hormonal development, emotion, and so forth.

Dopamine—working in consort with serotonin, oxytocin, and endorphins—is the agent that is released at the prospect of pleasure. It's the chemical that keeps us motivated to go after good-feeling things and keep the painful ones at bay. It's basically a reward system, responding to stimuli and sending waves of pleasantness to the parts of your brain that need it.

One of the things dopamine positively loves is the attainment of goals. When you finally achieve something you've been meaning to complete—anything from a crossword puzzle to a successful product launch—dopamine is released in spades, pent up in anticipation of your accomplishments. The more you do and accomplish, the better you feel. We want it as much as possible.

In fact, that's the problem.

We want dopamine so much that it damages our toughness. We are always seeking short-term gratification and the pleasure it creates. We are just not wired to delay gratification; rather, we are wired give in to the path of least resistance—in other words, the mentally *weak* path. When we are instantly rewarded, we are reinforced to continue on that path. When we engage in something that seems to provide only a distant promise of reward, it becomes much more difficult to adhere. Our biological imperative is to take the easy and pleasurable path over the *right* path.

But it doesn't have to be that way. There are a few ways that you can increase the flow of dopamine to be more constant, which will allow you to make the tough choice over the easy choice more consistently. This probably isn't your conception of toughness—to have to string your brain along as if it was a carrot dangling in front of a horse. And ideally, this process of dopamine manipulation isn't needed later on, but to start with, we must work within the confines of biology.

Picture yourself as a human lab rat. B.F. Skinner was a psychologist who studied behavior, and his "Skinner box"—technically termed an "operant conditioning chamber"—was a small chamber in which he used to experiment with rodents in the 1930s. Skinner's objective was to make rats behave in a certain way by administering pleasure as a reward. This is known in psychology circles as *behaviorism*. It gives a very clear view as to the effects of positive reinforcement on any animal, rat or human.

Here's how it worked: inside the Skinner box was a bar that, when pressed by the rodent, gave them food or water. The rat was not made aware of this action ahead of time—really, there's no good way to explain it to a rat—but rather, it was accidentally discovered it when they bumped into or depressed the bar and a morsel of food came flying out of a chute. The rat was impressed with this development and soon came to realize that every time he hit the bar, he'd get fed. So he did it more and more often. In this way, the rat's behavior was conditioned through positive reinforcement.

What does this have to do with manipulating dopamine to create lasting mental toughness? *Become the rat.*

Whenever you need help staying with something you'd really rather give up on, think of the task as that lever in the Skinner box. Make a tangible connection to an action and the subsequent reward, even if it is not immediate or significant. Visualize it. Feel it. Chew on the thought. Think through every little detail about it that appeals to you. Build a clear relationship with staying tough and a subsequent reward. Just the anticipation will work up your dopamine reserves and push you through to the end. And then, of course, after finishing a goal, dopamine will be released again.

I'll acknowledge this mental exercise might sound a little ridiculous, but the part of your brain that regulates dopamine absolutely *loves* this. The thing is, the brain doesn't care if the reward is visualized, imagined, or real—it's all the same to the brain and makes toughness easier to bear. Mind over matter, so to speak.

This is akin to *the placebo effect*, in which patients suffering from a certain condition are given sugar pills that they're told have restorative or curative powers when actually they're just sugar pills with no medically beneficial ingredients whatsoever. Regardless, some patients who were given sugar pills reported feeling a lot better anyway—leading researchers to believe that the placebo effect had value as a therapeutic tool. We'll touch on this more in Chapter 4.

The expectation that improvement or success is imminent creates a certain belief structure. If one sincerely believes in their own effectiveness, the trust that their efforts will result in real achievement, the brain responds by making subtle changes to our body chemistry that alleviate suffering or pain—namely, it ramps up dopamine production.

Even without a certified result, anticipation and expectation of one can stir up dopamine production. While this may sound on the surface like "selling" your brain an illusion, it really isn't. It's visualizing the potential success of your endeavors, which is a common technique many people use to get through work and reach real accomplishments. It's exactly that kind of expectation that fuels the fire of the tenacious.

In a similar vein, reframe the way you think about what you're facing. Instead of dreading the action of pressing the lever, associate it with only the positive gains you'll reap.

People who push their way through adverse conditions and get things done are often praised as having tremendous willpower, which, on balance, is a good thing. But not everybody has that unlimited supply of determination at their disposal.

Using our grit and resolve to get through a chore isn't considered pleasant. Quite the opposite, in fact: "perseverance" is more associated with "pain." When you're using all your resources to get through a task, there are trace levels of discomfort, anxiety, and even a little physical strain being put upon you. Even if it's mild or barely noticeable, it's there. Your body and brain would really rather get through this uncomfortable circumstance and head straight for the next somewhat pleasurable thing.

Pleasure and anticipation create dopamine, so the trick is making effort and work feel less like a matter of will and more like something pleasant.

Gym rats do this all the time. When they first started working out, they might have found the effort to get more physical activity a little difficult to do and therefore not pleasant. But they managed to push through it because, for them, the process of working out has become something to look forward to: "Sweat equals bliss." Every time they bench press 250 pounds, they *enjoy* it. Probably because they've already seen some results of their work that have been positive.

You can consciously turn what seems like slogging through menial work into a pleasant experience. Rather than picturing studying as a long and tedious process, reframe it as something that will eventually bring a positive result—won't it be *fun* to be smarter? This part I'll warrant is a bit like selling your brain on a lie. But it's a *helpful* lie for the greater good.

If it's still hard for you to imagine work as being fun, you can make some minor adjustments to actually make the situation more comfortable. If you're facing a mountain of drudgery at work, consider ways to make the process more comfortable, whether it's music, conversation, or something you enjoy listening to.

Just picturing work as an opportunity for enjoyment has more effect on your drive to accomplish something than grunting up your willpower and vowing to struggle. Next thing you know, you'll be a tenacious beast, but you were having too much fun to notice.

Changes in attitude and mental direction are one thing—theoretically, they're easier for some to execute because it requires internal mind power. But there are also systematic techniques we can use to help stimulate dopamine production and drive motivation upward.

Give yourself deadlines. Put yourself on a schedule for completing individual tasks throughout the day. Make all your projects due at a specific time: working out, finishing a paper, researching—even housecleaning or walking the dog. And then stick to those deadlines. Dopamine release is especially responsive to timed obligations, so anticipation of the end of a certain time limit will increase its production.

However, it's important that you not turn that deadline-generated rush of dopamine into a regular habit that you depend on to get things finished. Leaving everything until the last possible minute just to stimulate excitement to drive you toward completion can boomerang back in very unpleasant ways. Instead, break your big, huge deadline into a series of smaller, spaced-out, more easily achievable ones. Even these reduced-scale deadlines can generate dopamine production—and the more achievements you make, even if they're minor ones, the more often this process will take place.

Break down big barriers into small blocks. Similarly, when we see a sizable obstacle in our path to success, we tend to develop an attitude that we need to get rid of it all at once.

This is the equivalent of feeling good only when you finish 100% of a task and only serves to delay your gratification and weaken yourself. Instead, break the obstacle down into individual chunks: smaller components that make up the bigger problem at hand and are much easier to tackle one by one. More dopamine more frequently.

The Toughness Résumé

I'd like to end this opening chapter with a little exercise that's akin to writing a résumé to apply for a new job, only instead of marketable job skills and your education, you'll be listing out just how tough you are and when these occasions happened. In a sense, you are selling you to yourself.

This is to change the narrative you have told yourself for years. The voice in your head has been a negative one, telling you what you can't do and why you're not strong enough. But it's wrong, and this simple list is evidence of that. Taking inventory allows you to gain an accurate look at yourself, which will help minimize your weaknesses and normalize your strengths. In short, you will feel permission to see yourself in a tougher, more positive light than before.

By gaining an objective and realistic view of what you are capable of, you can base your confidence on what is real instead of what is imagined. No matter how demoralized or weak you feel today, always remember what you've done in the past. That's the type of person you objectively are. Nothing has changed to separate you from the person you were that day to the current day where you feel low.

The toughness résumé isn't a checklist of things you should tell others; rather, it's for yourself.

When you have this résumé created, you'll be able to glance at it and instantly know that you're not the type of person you feel you are at the moment. You're more than that. You're above it, and you have the evidence right in front of you. Every single item on the résumé is a *fact* about yourself, but you've probably suppressed or ignored them while constructing your negative self-narrative.

This is the information that shows you just how great you are, what you've done, the type of person you are, and how impressive you can be. If brainstorming this information was difficult, it's a sign that you probably have an *extremely* negative view of yourself. By having your résumé ready for action, you'll be able to battle your inner demons any time you feel low.

It won't be easy to come up with these on the fly, but that's precisely why it's so important to construct this résumé beforehand. You won't be able to think of these immediately, and some of these are buried so deep in your brain they'll never come up organically.

So what exactly goes into the toughness résumé? This is just a guide; you can come up with your own list, but this works for me and is a great place to start.

- 10 toughest accomplishments
- 5 toughest experiences
- 5 tough things you've done that no one else has
- 5 tough things you can do that no one else can

You get the idea. You can keep going, but what we're doing here is taking inventory of your best hits and making them easy to refer to. That's 25 pieces of real evidence that, even if you feel like you are constantly faltering, you are capable of so much more. Believing is where we must start.

Looking at the list, which will naturally become impressive and interesting, you can start to realize the type of person you actually are. This is the conclusion the evidence leads to. Any other conclusion is in your head.

Take the time to write these out and go over them regularly. I even encourage people to write them on an index card and carry it around with them as a confidence boost whenever they are contemplating whether they have it within them to persevere or not give up. You've done it before, and you can do it again!

Takeaways:

- Toughness is simply one of the keys to life. It gets you wherever you want to go, and it accurately realizes that the biggest obstacle in life is yourself. If we aren't able to embody toughness and persevere through hardships, we will inevitably end up on Someday Isle. That is not a pleasant vacation spot; it's more of a purgatory where people go when they've given up. And it's tough to escape.
- Toughness is sabotaged by a few toxic patterns of thought. These include cynicism, negativism, defeatism, escapism, and delayism.
- Dopamine is one of the most important aspects of toughness. We lack toughness because we seek the instant gratification of dopamine. This causes us to give up, binge, relax, and otherwise make the easy or pleasurable choice over the

correct and tougher choice. We want dopamine too much and too frequently. We can battle this by using the placebo effect, using a positive spin, giving yourself deadlines, and breaking down tasks to create greater feelings of accomplishment.

- The toughness résumé is something for your eyes only. It's a reminder of just how tough you've been in your life, whether willingly or not. This will change the narrative of who you are as a person—what's on the résumé is who you are, and that's hard evidence! Use this to stay tough in difficult times when all you want to do is throw in the towel and give up. You've faced worse and lived, so you can face the current day as well.

Chapter 2. Your Excuses Are Lies

A winner is just a loser who tried one more time. – George Augustus Moore

Brett would *love* to start his own tourism business. He's been working for a big corporation his entire life, and he's tired of answering to other people and making money for someone else.

He's got the idea to start an operation that provides Hawaiian tourists a complete land-and-water experience of the islands. But not just the same places every Hawaiian tourist visits. He'll show them the *hidden gems* of Hawaii, the places only locals know about. He'll tell them unheard stories and aboriginal folklore that will stimulate their imaginations. This would be the *real Hawaii* that only those with ancestors going back hundreds of years would see. Great idea!

But in the midst of daydreaming about this idea, Brett becomes aware of some "harsh realities." He doesn't know the first thing about tour vehicles. What kind of licenses does he need to get? It was hard enough getting his driver's license—how is he going to actually get a *specialized* one? That's too hard.

Besides, Brett thinks, why does everybody go to Hawaii in the first place? To surf, sunbathe, or drink. Nobody goes to Hawaii to learn more about its culture, Brett reasons. That's why people go to *Europe*, not Hawaii. What island visitor cares about what he would have to offer? It's too difficult to figure out.

And another thing, Brett realizes: all small businesses have it tough. Most of them fail. It's a huge risk to sink money into an independent business. All that marketing research, setting up shop, getting equipment, advertising—Brett can't do that kind of stuff. There's no way he could learn all of it in time to get started. He's an idea guy, and the execution part has always intimidated him.

Forget it, Brett says to himself. It was a lousy idea. There's no way he can pull all of it off. It's just too much work and he's not sure where to start. He's just going to stay in his current job and keep safe and secure. Brett suddenly hears his mailbox clink. He goes outside to find just one piece of mail in it—a postcard with a picture of a gray cubicle with miserable-looking drones filing out.

Above the picture is a message: "Greetings from Someday Isle. See you soon!"

The Psychology of Excuses

Brett was just another victim of the Someday Isle phenomenon—fated to always fall short of his true destination and end up on Someday Isle for a lack of toughness. For most of us, Brett included, excuses are at the root of our lack of toughness and why we end up there.

Excuses are reflexive and instinctual ways in which we justify negative occurrences. Excuses are what we present when we don't want to do something or something doesn't go our way. They shift blame. Whether it's your fault or not, your initial impulse is often to find a way to deflect responsibility onto anything but you.

"It's the copy machine's fault," "The other driver was moving too slow," "The reading material was too hard to understand," "The ring (from Lord of the Rings) was supposed to prevent me from aging."

But here's the thing; excuses are categorically lies. It's a harsh truth that needs to be exposed in order for you to become more accountable and get where you want to go. Not just 99% of excuses, and not just the ones that other people use. *All* of them are lies that deprive you of mental toughness and the ability to cope with reality. Of course, there are always *reasons* things go wrong, but you'll read soon how vastly reasons differ from excuses.

We think of excuses as things we tell other people—parents, bosses, teachers, spouses, police officers—to protect our image or standing. And they are. When you tell excuses to other people, you're not necessarily hurting yourself. Others may grow annoyed at you and question your sense of responsibility, but that can be somewhat overcome.

But the people we make the most excuses to, almost without exception, are ourselves. While we tell excuses to others so we don't look bad in their eyes, we tell excuses to ourselves to protect our own ego and self-esteem. This is by far the more important function of constant excuses, and unfortunately, it leads to living in a fantasy world where any reason for toughness is simply excused away.

To be more specific, this is when excuses become a *defense mechanism*, which was first coined in the setting of psychoanalytic therapy. Over time, it became so recognized and prevalent that it's part of our common, daily language.

Defense mechanisms are unconscious, psychological reactions that rationalize or ease our anxiety. They protect us from the unpleasantness of confronting our weakness and flaws. They guard us from having to deal with threats, challenges, or anything else we don't want to think about. They make us feel better about ourselves.

A major part of building toughness is to understand your flaws so you can address them—excuses rob you of this ability, leaving you stranded in disempowering thoughts. When you tell yourself excuses, you're not just indulging in small acts of self-preservation. You're making yourself a permanent victim, with little to no agency in your own actions. Without looking at yourself critically and to protect your ego, you are letting yourself make the same mistakes over and over again.

Excuses are refusing to keep going when the going gets tough. Excuses are when you get knocked down and find a reason to stay down. *Excuses are giving up*.

Generally, if the first priority of what you're saying is to make clear how you are *not* involved, you're using an excuse, *which is a lie*. It's an easy habit to slip into unconsciously. Once you figure out that it feels great to not have to take responsibility for yourself, you'll start using it more and more until you can't tell the difference between the excuse and reality.

Everyone makes excuses, and you'd think the people who make excuses to themselves the most are those with low self-esteem. In reality, people with *high* (or externally high, anyway) self-esteem use excuses the most to maintain their own egos. Think of it this way: the higher the self-esteem, the longer and more painful the fall if it all comes crashing down.

The consequences of constant excuses are something Professor Sean McCrea of the University of Konstanz, Germany, calls *self-handicapping*. It is aptly named because that's exactly what making excuses is: reinforcing your belief in your *inability* to do something.

McCrea's experiments were conducted in three phases on groups of university students. In the first session, students took a test, were told how they scored, and were asked about how much effort they put into preparing for the test. They also indicated how they planned to prepare for a future test.

The next two sessions were a bit different. In the second, the students took an intelligence test. They were also told it would be especially helpful if they practiced before the test, but then they were split into two groups: one that would have the chance to practice and another that wouldn't.

That's when the researchers started playing mind games. They told each group they had to switch groups because of a computer error that mixed them up. This was a lie—generated strictly because it gave the (new) non-practice group the opportunity to make an excuse in case they performed poorly. So now the practice group (which was originally the non-practice group) got a chance to practice. The non-practice group (who were originally the practice group) did not.

After all this, everybody took the test. But the researchers had another trick up their sleeves: they told *every* student that they only scored 30% on the test, regardless of how they really did. Finally, the students were asked how they felt about their results.

The remaining session was similar to the last session, with a couple of twists. Sixty-six students were told they would be taking a math test that would also measure their logical abilities. They were also told they had to do short practice tests or else the evaluation wouldn't be accurate, so each student had either a short or long practice session. Each student then took the test, and again, the researchers told them they scored poorly, regardless of their actual scores.

The students were asked about their performance. But in this round, they were asked how strongly they agreed or disagreed with 10 already-prepared responses. Many of the prepared responses were, as you might expect, excuses: "If I'd practiced, I would have done better."

In the last phase of this session (stick with me here), the students were told there would be a *second* test—surprise!—and that practice would definitely be beneficial. They were given the opportunity to practice for 10 minutes but weren't forced to do so. Finally, the researchers let the subjects know the whole part about the second test was just a ruse; there wouldn't actually be one. They then asked the students how they felt and if they really thought practice would help them.

If you got lost in the description of the admittedly complex study, here's the important part. The results of all these sessions were, ultimately, the same.

In the first study, students who didn't put a lot of effort into studying cited that as a reason they didn't do well ("If I would have worked harder, I would have succeeded"). This was described as *upward counterfactual* thinking: envisioning a positive result if a certain condition was met. But further reflections were contingent upon the student's level of self-esteem. Those with low self-regard were more motivated to study in the future, but those with somewhat bigger egos generally said they didn't intend to prepare too hard the next time—because they had an excuse ready.

The results of the more complicated second and third studies reinforced that point and revealed a few more. Students who didn't get enough practice also expressed upward counterfactual thinking. Those who *had* practiced reported negative self-esteem when they heard their scores (remember, everybody was told they performed the same). But those who hadn't practiced showed no effect to their self-esteem—in other words, they felt exactly the same and didn't feel motivated to change their practice habits. Again, they had cover for the future: an excuse.

What does this all mean? That excuses do more than just keep people blameless: they can also reduce their motivation to work harder in the future. Excuses can give cover for having lower expectations of yourself. They can even make a bad result look positive ("But I had so many things working against me—this is about as good as it gets!"). People are also more likely to use excuses to shift blame onto others, even if the failures are strictly their own fault.

Even though excuses make for great initial cover-ups, they are the linchpin of an unconscious strategy we sometimes use to absolve ourselves of blame in *future* efforts. That scheme is called *self-handicapping*, but you know it better as "I can't fail if I don't try!"

Self-Handicapping

The ways excuses provide cover for one's insufficiency are many and insidious. As mentioned before, excuses are the epitome of giving up. In fact, excuses cause giving up in the future as well as in the current situation.

The self-handicapper, knowingly or not, places obstacles in their own path to getting something accomplished. They make these handicaps known, at least to themselves, and probably to others. That way if they fail, they can just blame it all on the handicap instead of their own ineptitude. But if the project is a success, then they can claim *more* credit than they might deserve, because they had to overcome all these terrible odds that were stacked against them. (Alternately, if they're successful, they may become terribly confused as to *why* they succeeded, causing great cognitive dissonance and making progress much more difficult.)

Self-handicapping is like an emotional insurance policy. No matter the outcome, the person is protected from negative responsibility. They're shielded from all the upshots of failure—it's not *their* fault all these barriers were in their way (though it kind of is).

For example, a student may know his biology final is coming up, but the night before he goes to a bar and has a few too many giant punchbowls of alcohol. If his final comes back with a low grade, he blames it on his decision to party the night before. He didn't truly give it his best, so he doesn't have to feel badly about failing.

The supposed reasons one self-handicaps turn out to be quite counter-productive. The presence of self-imposed barriers can put a cap on future success and toughness in the face of adversity. In fact, no adversity will be faced at all.

Indeed, most habitual self-handicappers prove to be objectively low achievers who can't adapt to changing circumstances or challenging environments. That ability to adjust to shifting or difficult conditions is a prime quality of the mentally tough. For the tenacious, there's no room for self-handicapping or excuses in their mindset, especially when situations are always in flux.

Even though the damage is mostly to the self, self-handicapping does create a significant backlash from others. Excuses tend to be transparent whines, and nobody's really concerned with all the reasons they *can't* do something. Giving excuses and disclaimers isn't really a resounding endorsement of the self-handicapper's abilities. Indeed, according to McCrea, self-handicappers tend to get lower grades, run higher risks of alcoholism, and have trouble in social situations.

For example, let's say someone has a huge presentation at work that they're tasked to prepare. What might their internal dialogue sound like? Nervous about their chances, they procrastinate working on it until the last possible minute. No matter what happens, they're covered. If the presentation bombs, they'll feel secure that it's because they put it off too long (which is, most likely, very true). This protects their ego because they won't have to analyze why their best effort still resulted in failure. It's classic self-handicapping behavior because they sabotage themselves and don't take responsibility.

Self-handicapping comes in various forms: low effort or preparation, not getting sleep, exaggerated physical problems, setting unrealistic goals, even bashfulness. It consists of anything that can provide a kind of disclaimer to potential failure, which also neatly overlaps with escaping responsibility and having to practice discipline or perseverance.

Excuses vs. Reasons

So are there legitimate *reasons* that things can go wrong?

Telling the difference between an *excuse* and a *reason*, admittedly, can be tricky. In general, it comes down to one's ability to take responsibility for whatever they contribute—or fail to contribute—to a failed effort or mistake.

Excuses are intended to shift blame and allow us to give up. To use an excuse is to live in one's own weakness and helplessness. Reasons, on the other hand, focus squarely on our own actions, behaviors, and decision-making. They reinforce responsibility and lead more directly to possible change. Reasons are when you don't give up and you make the effort to push through your pain.

Of course, this doesn't mean that external factors *never* play a part in real reasons; there are always elements outside our immediate control that can affect an outcome. But a legitimate reason centers our own roles in the situation and acknowledges the mistakes or misjudgments we made that prevented optimal results from happening. They spotlight the control we have in a situation. Although admitting one's shortcoming can seem like a failing, it makes it easier to diagnose what's going wrong and make adjustments in the future. Excuses simply don't bring that kind of information or toughness to light.

Although one should always try to accept as much responsibility as one can, sometimes excuses are unavoidable. While you should always be careful when explaining the uncontrollable outside factors that lead to undesired results, certain excuses are indeed better than others. Researcher David B. Weiner identified three aspects that generally make for, if not a great excuse, a plausible one.

External factors. The weather and traffic excuses from the first example are unavoidable—and even if, in normal situations, you should be able to plan around them, sometimes you simply won't be able to. Even "better" is when an inanimate object is the cause of your downfall: "My car didn't start," "The computer suddenly froze," "An asteroid fell on my bus stop." You can't punish an inanimate object, so the whole blame game is taken out of the equation.

Uncontrollable factors. These are situations where you have no capacity to control how events unfolded. Perhaps you weren't present where the mitigating factor occurred ("The print shop where the reports were being printed was evacuated due to a fire") or you had no reasonable jurisdiction over events that contributed to the failure ("Serena's husband left her last night, and she was quite reasonably unprepared to be here today") or unexpected health issues came about ("I had appendicitis"). The further away you are from the center of control over the situation, the less you're responsible for it.

That's a fair point but should be carefully considered before you explain it to make sure you really *didn't* have control over the situation.

Unintended factors. A person's responsibility in a misdeed is directly tied into what their intentions were. If one admits they intended to do something (or not do something), then that makes them look like terrible people. Although you can backhandedly admire the forthrightness of someone who *admits* they meant to do something wrong ("I slashed your tires because I don't like your attitude"), a "good" excuse is absent of bad purposes or ill will. "I forgot to put a stamp on my tax returns" or "I made a mistake counting how much money we had in the budget" are—if a bit lame—not horrifyingly bad excuses. At least they *sound* honest.

Let's say you arrived late for an important meeting. Perhaps the culprits were a combination of heavy traffic, bad weather, or a personal phone call that went longer than you expected and kept you from getting ready. There are two ways you can

63

present this. You could bemoan the fact that the weather, traffic, and call are out of your control—these are excuses. Or you could say you didn't consult traffic reports, weather reports, or set a boundary on the length of the phone call—these are reasons.

Will giving reasons guarantee that you'll escape others' temporary scorn or mental judgment? Not necessarily. But taking responsibility and emphasizing your agency in the matter is what transforms you from someone who gets knocked down and waits for help into someone who gets knocked down and finds a way to claw themselves up. In the end, you are the only one who can force yourself to keep going when it gets difficult. Your toughness determines your life, not how lucky you are with traffic or weather.

For another example, let's say you led a team that was tasked with delivering a class project—and it didn't go well. The research was questionable at best and the delivery was uneven and sounded ill-informed. It was met with waves of dismissive silence.

What are your options for establishing why things went south? Well, you could throw everybody else under the bus and claim they didn't do their part. You could say your online research didn't turn up a lot of valuable information. You could also say the topic was impossible to do a concise report about and that nobody else could have done it either. All these are excuses—and pretty terrible ones at that.

What if you expressed your sorrows to recognize more responsibility? You could say you didn't effectively look for alternative means of research in the time you were given, that you failed to delegate certain functions to the rest of your team, or that you needed to be more realistic about choosing a topic that's possible to cover, keep its scope within certain limits, and try not to over-promise what you may not be able to deliver. Not only do all of those reasons explain your part in the situation, but they're also things within your control that you can improve on in the future.

It's unpleasant and it might even be temporarily depressing, but the realization that your excuses are lies is instrumental to mental toughness. No, they aren't reasons, and no, they aren't legitimate. Their primary purpose is to let you feel more comfortable by giving up. But we're in the real world, so buckle up for the bumpy ride.

Common Excuses

Making excuses isn't always a deliberate thing. In fact, most of the time we state excuses, they're coming from a certain mindset or personality profile that we've developed over time. This often makes it hard to pinpoint exactly when we use excuses because we tend toward certain ways of thinking that we just accept as "who we are."

Some of these mindsets are classic personality types that we're all familiar with to an extent. Others are patterns of thought that we don't easily recognize. All of them conspire to make us delay, procrastinate, or simply refuse to do something. But they're also correctable.

There are many different mindsets that contribute to the act of excuse-making, but we'll focus on five of the more common ones. You may recognize a small overlap with the saboteurs of toughness from the previous chapter.

The Perfectionist. This is someone who only acknowledges results if everything goes exactly as they planned. There can be no deviation whatsoever. The Perfectionist takes a stark "all-or-nothing" approach to what they see done: either everything is right or absolutely nothing gets done. And of course, you can bet the standards of a Perfectionist are frequently impossible to meet. They'll have an absolute floor of expectation—if that minimum level of accomplishment isn't meant, the entire project is a waste. So why bother?

How to change the Perfectionist mindset? First, stop thinking of accomplishments as "off/on" switches, where there's just the binary of "done/not done." Rather, think of efforts in terms of a "dial," where all efforts are simply measured in levels of intensity. You might be going at 85%, 50%, or 3%—

but you're doing *something* instead of shutting down if things aren't perfectly executed. Something is better than nothing. If you don't come out of the gate stronger than anyone else and do everything perfectly, you can always adjust along the way. It's a fluid process.

The Intimidated. People with this mindset have some commonalities with the Perfectionist, in that they use an "ideal condition" to gauge the effectiveness of their efforts. But the Intimidated is more gripped with fear than the Perfectionist. They're afraid they've overshot their ability and have taken on more than they can handle. The Intimidated is driven by a consumptive fear of the unknown and the prospect of total failure. Not only will the results be bad, but they'll also be downright disastrous—the cake in the oven won't just burn; you'll set the entire kitchen on fire.

To tame the Intimidated and overcome your terror of what might happen, the answer's very simple: research. Consider what's the worst-case scenario in your efforts: what would truly define utter catastrophe? Write the answer down and make whatever plans and reinforcements you need to avoid that terrible event from unfolding—and then get to work.

Remember too that failure is something to *learn* from. Just allowing yourself to be defined by failure, without trying to figure out the adjustments you could make to achieve a better result, is a lifelong recipe for eternal procrastination. Resist the urge to overthink and over-analyze in advance and risk "analysis paralysis"—just start something.

The Environment Blamer. People with this mindset are completely at the mercy of their surroundings. They believe they have no input or control about what happens. Life to them is merely a sequence of things that happen to them, not the accomplishments they make. Their belief that outside forces are always conspiring against them leads them to focus only on the external and not at all on their own internal abilities or contributions. This is especially helpful when they're trying to evade responsibility.

To change the environment-blaming mindset, simply accept accountability and realize that things don't have to happen *to you*. Understand that you have just as much ability to affect your surroundings as anyone or anything else. Nothing prevents you from doing so besides yourself. This is a matter of understanding just how much you can participate in your daily life. Question whether the environment is really the cause of your sorrows or whether it's just a convenient excuse. Like the example from earlier, traffic and weather might happen to you, but that doesn't mean you can't account for them yourself.

The Defeatist. This mindset is pessimistic. A Defeatist is certain there's no chance for success—and won't let you forget about it. They've already decided they're not going to succeed, whether they say so or not. The Defeatist uses their lack of optimism to explain their own inabilities—it's not really a reflection of the truth, just that they lack the requisite tools to do anything. More often than not, this attitude stops being an opinion and turns into a self-fulfilling prophecy: they really *will* start stinking at everything.

To change the Defeatist mindset, stop confirming your own failure. Even if it runs counter to your ideas of reality, just attack the problem you're trying to solve or the goal you're trying to achieve. Break the big task down into smaller and more manageable pieces—try to score a few "quick wins" instead of the league championship all at once. It's fair and even prudent to expect hardships or tough stretches, and it's even okay to ask for outside assistance. Just don't declare that failure is inevitable. It's never a done deal.

Excuse-making is the most temporary and fruitless method to feel better. Rather than repair faults and flaws from the ground up, an excuse is more like a Band-Aid that just obscures flaws and does little to fix them. Understanding the nature of excuses helps us see them coming before we speak them. That pause in our thinking can help us see what the *real* situation is and can open up insights into how we can positively affect them. And that leads to a tenacious character that can contend with anything that comes down the path.

Reframe Your Excuses

Now that we understand the true purpose of excuses and why they are so unhelpful, it's time to learn a method to deal with them as they arise.

The solution isn't necessarily to deny what we're telling ourselves, as that's nearly impossible. Excuses reflect certain states of mind that we may indeed *think* we're experiencing. Instead of denying your excuses, try to dig below the surface and find three components*: the truth, the mentally weak conclusion, and the mentally tough conclusion.* Drawing a clear distinction between these three factors is what will allow you to truly understand your internal dialogue and isolate where you can choose to be tough and resilient.

For example, let's say you have an essay that's due in a few days that will require you to perform research. You have a reasonable window of time to get it completed—but you're exhausted—this is the truth. This is the neutral reality of the situation. This is where the fork in the road appears and you will make your choice about how to approach it—with toughness or not.

Now ask yourself what an excuse for the truth would sound like. This might be your first impulse—to come up with an excuse *not* to get started. "I could start now, but I'll do much better after I get some sleep." There's your *mentally weak* conclusion: it's allowing you to procrastinate. Even though there might be a hint of truth, its sole purpose is to allow you to take the easy way out. It is indisputably the path of least resistance. It seems to be small and harmless, but it is actually attempting to absolve you of responsibility.

Then ask yourself what the best approach for the truth is. On the other hand, you could say, "I'm tired, but if nothing else I can do a few small things right now to get the paper going. I could make a rough outline that'll make this paper easier to navigate when I'm more refreshed." That's a *mentally tough* conclusion. It is recognizing what the right and most effective choice is instead of the easy choice. It doesn't demand that you exhaust yourself, but it ensures that you set yourself up for success.

Often, it's only when we engage in this type of role-playing that we can understand we are even making an excuse. You're not required to *reject* the conditions that make up your mentally weak conclusions. No, it's not about becoming a relentless machine in the face of all adversity. Step by step, it's just about realizing that you have many choices and that the choices that lead to toughness are just a slight pivot away.

In a sense, whatever you make an excuse about is something that belongs on your to-do list. It's exactly what you should focus your attention on. If you think you don't have time, then you've probably got a time management problem. If you like to say that you're just unlucky, learn about people who have had good luck. If you feel that you are singled out for negative treatment from a supervisor, then you may very well need to improve your office social skills. We can move forward only when we realize that excuses are lies.

Takeaways:

- Let's get this out of the way up front: excuses are lies. Excuses are the very epitome of giving up in the face of adversity, because excuses create a reality where adversity doesn't exist. They are the easy way out and lead you down a path of learned helplessness and playing the victim.

- Even worse, excuses lead to self-handicapping, which is otherwise known as "I can't fail if I don't try." Not only is that detrimental to toughness, but it also drags down your entire outlook to life.

- Some excuses are real, and we distinguish them by calling them reasons. Reasons are focused on your personal responsibility and agency in a matter. Reasons epitomize toughness because they recognize a hardship and choose to look at it straight on and persevere.

- Common excuse patterns include playing the perfectionist, blaming the environment, being too intimidated, and being a defeatist. A method to defeat these excuse patterns, as well as any other excuses in general, is to look for three components of your situation: the truth, the mentally weak conclusion, and the mentally strong conclusion. Finding the separation between these perspectives is how you can realize which path you should take.

Chapter 3. Strategize Against Apathy, Weakness, and Giving Up

A river cuts through a rock not because of its power, but its persistence. – Jim Watkins

Dora has the greatest idea for a historical novel: a Renaissance love triangle. She doesn't know how it's going to go yet, but it involves a romantic poet, an infantryman who's close to retiring, and the bar maiden who serves them both. She's started a first draft and has three chapters down.

But she's at a point where she doesn't really know where the plot's going to go. One afternoon she sits down to try and figure it out. The effort is a bit forced. She figures she can use a few minutes to recharge and walks away from her laptop. She'll get back to it soon enough.

Six hours of social media later, Dora's gotten so removed from the creative mindset that she decides she's just going to delay for the rest of the day. She has some busy work to do in the living room anyway. Her back issues of *The Paris Review* need to be sorted and there's a wine stain on the carpet she needs to get out.

A week goes by. Dora's day job is putting more pressure on her. She's nowhere close to a creative state of mind. Besides, she thinks, maybe the busy work she has to complete will help get her excited about starting up with the novel again.

A month and a half go by. Dora's miserable because she's completely immersed in matters at work that really don't interest her in the slightest. And she's forgotten about her novel. There doesn't seem to be any point in going back to it now; there are bills to pay and matters that need her attention.

A year goes by and Dora hasn't even opened her story file in eight months. She's forgotten all about it, until one day when she sees the *New York Times* bestseller list and notices that the #1 book for five weeks is something called *The Fire-Eyed Maid: A Renaissance Love Triangle.* It's been optioned for film rights even though reviews have been middling. Dora finds a copy of the book at a local retailer, thumbs through it, and says to herself, "I could have written this in my sleep!"

Then she realizes she had the chance but kept putting it off and losing interest.

Bummed beyond belief, she looks at the author bio in the back of the book. It's the author's first novel after writing fan fiction about *The Tudors* for nine months. The bio says the author "lives with her husband, two children, and six parrots in the seaside community of... *Someday Isle*." Alas, that's where Dora was also destined to end up after failing to toughen up in times of adversity.

There are very few processes in the world that don't benefit from planning. Such is the case with building toughness. Even though it's a mental process employing brain power, having a blueprint for achieving toughness will make the whole process clearer and simpler. This chapter reveals some approaches and methods you can put into practice that will help you build tenacity more effectively and possibly even more quickly.

How vs. Why

Many of us are analytical by habit. Think of this as a prelude to the rest of the chapter. Before we take action or put a plan into motion, we spend a fair amount of time questioning our motives and our desired goals: *why* exactly do we want what we want? It's easy to spend a lot of time in the state of "why," because it can be intellectually engaging. And thinking about the "why" certainly has some advantages in terms of personal awareness. This can be endless, and after a certain amount of time, you're not any closer to dealing with your problem.

It's inactive. At some point there's no need to keep looking for reasons or analyzing your motives or ambitions. When someone decides to start a fitness regimen, they're probably clear on their reasons why: they want to get healthier, they want to lose weight, they want to get stronger. The potential results are very appealing. Knowing all these reasons doesn't take care of the actual nuts and bolts of the fitness program: getting out to the gym, making meal plans, scheduling jobs, avoiding rich desserts for a while, or anything practical.

At some point you'll have enough justification for taking a certain course of action. That's when it's time to stop asking "why" and starting planning "how." "How" questions address the specifics of how to attain the goals we set for ourselves. Without arranging and executing the step-by-step procedures of a plan, the "why" becomes insignificant.

"Why" questions can be important down the line. If we find ourselves stumbling or growing weary of sticking to the program, occasionally we'll have to remind ourselves what our reasons were for getting into it in the first place. That's a fair time to go back over the whys. But as soon as is practical, it's important to get back to work. Otherwise, we run the risk of letting our "why" self-questions become another excuse to stop moving forward.

This chapter is therefore full of "how."

Visualization: Seeing Is Believing

A powerful tool that's often overlooked is *visualization*. This happens before you lift a finger and is something that you can repeat ad nauseam to build mental toughness and quit the habit of giving up. We mentioned it earlier in the book in the context of manipulating dopamine, but there's much more to it.

Visualization, quite simply put, is *detailed imagination*. You use your mind's eye to picture yourself executing whatever it is you're planning to accomplish. Visualization helps you build a sense of awareness and expectation. It's a mental rehearsal to understand the experience and associated emotions.

And believe it or not, it works. Australian researcher Alan Richardson ran a trial on visualization on a group of basketball players. He divided them into three different groups and gave each a 20-day assignment involving free throws.

All of the groups physically practiced making free throws on the first and last days of the 20-day period. One group was instructed to practice making free throws for 20 minutes every day. A second group was instructed to do nothing in between the first and twentieth days.

Finally, a third group was told only to "visualize" themselves making free throws between the first and last days of the trials. This process didn't just mean the players pictured themselves sinking shots successfully—it also included visualizing their *missing* free throws and *practicing* correcting their shot.

The results were eye-opening. The group that physically practiced for 20 days boosted their free throw success rate by 24%. But astonishingly, the visualization group also improved by 23%—almost as much as the practice squad. Not surprisingly, the group that did neither didn't improve at all.

The conclusion from this study is that visualization causes changes even when unaccompanied by actual physical work. The brain and its neural pathways can be conditioned and strengthened, just as muscles and the cardiovascular system can. Visualization can help bring the brain into accord with the physical execution of anything we do and can be a great means of additional support in our efforts. Seeing is believing.

Can we visualize ourselves to be more resilient? Absolutely. Visualize a situation you are afraid of and make all the tough, disciplined, and unpleasant choices in your mind. Play it through with as many details as possible. How does it feel? We can start to understand that our fear is rooted in ignorance, and we can start to build a relationship with the feeling of comfort with discomfort. Almost all of us hesitate and want to retreat to a comfort zone when confronted with something foreign. Make risky situations as familiar as possible and this instinct will decrease accordingly.

Visualization is easy, but as with any process it works best with guided steps. It is helpful to approach visualization as meditation—a quiet but concentrated immersion into your thoughts and imagination. One particularly effective technique involves five steps.

1. Relaxation. The first step involves getting yourself into a tranquil state, physically and mentally. It involves techniques like finding a quiet spot, taking deep and measured breaths, and closing your eyes to get into a meditative state.

2. Imagining the environment. The second step is building a detailed mental picture of the situation, surroundings, and specific objects that you'll be working with when you finally take action.

3. Viewing as third person. The third part of this method is picturing yourself doing an activity the way someone else would—how you'd appear in the eyes of someone watching you.

4. Viewing as first person. The fourth part is an intensive imagining of yourself doing the activity—how your senses and emotions would react and feel while you're doing it.

5. Coming back to reality. The final part involves *slowly* reemerging from your visualization into the physical world, ready to take on the challenge for real.

Let's try a sample visualization with a situation that we frequently find ourselves in but can cause some to feel utter panic and terror about: delivering a speech. It doesn't seem as challenging as jumping out of an airplane or taking part in a sword fight, but some of the toughest people in the world have trepidation about standing in front of a group of polite people and speaking directly to them. Applying the above five steps, here's how that visualization might go.

1. Relax. Find a quiet spot where you won't be disturbed or interrupted for a few minutes—lying on a couch or bed with the windows and doors closed. Breathe deeply from your stomach. Take as much time as you need to let all areas of tension in your body dissipate. Finally, close your eyes.

2. Imagine the environment. Make a detailed survey of the room and space where you'll be making your speech. Picture the chairs the audience will sit in. Imagine the lighting and feel of the room, from how bright the overhead lamps might be to the air conditioning. Is the stage raised above the floor? Is there a podium you'll be standing behind? Will there be a microphone, or will you be wearing a headset? Imagine how either looks, down to the foam piece over the microphone head or the tiny earphones.

3. View as third person. Now you're somebody in the audience watching as you speak. You see yourself dressed in a suit, standing upright, delivering words clearly and directly, raising your pitch to make a point or lowering your pitch to make a joke. You're seeing all the hand gestures, head tilts, and facial expressions you'd see if you were watching the speech instead of giving it.

4. View as first person. At this point you go back into yourself, giving the speech and addressing the audience. You can hear how your words sound in your head. You note the distance from your mouth to the microphone. You can see the audience members' faces as they're paying attention. You hear the reverb from your voice echoing throughout the room, whether it's a little or a lot. You feel your hands resting on the wood surface of the podium. You see the words printed on the page you're reading from—or you see yourself moving around the stage without a script. You sense how your body's reacting: the nervous energy in your gut, the clarity in your head, the blood flow in your arms and legs. You hear the applause at the end, down to each individual handclap.

5. Wrap it up. You let the scene fade to black (or white if you prefer) in your head. You spend a few moments slowly coming back to, remembering the scene that's just transpired and marking each feeling you'll look out for when you're giving the speech. Recall specifically all the choices you made that were bold and daring as opposed to conservative and fearful. Then you gently open your eyes.

Somehow that visualization has made speech-giving seem terribly exciting. Imagine what it can do for parachuting and sword fighting.

We call the previously described process "visualization," but that phrasing isn't entirely accurate since most people associate visualization with seeing things with one's eyes. It happens. A more exact term for this process might be *multi-sensory imagination* or *mental rehearsal,* because the full process draws from all of the senses we possess:

Visual: sense of sight

Auditory: sense of hearing

Kinesthetic: sense of touch

Olfactory: sense of smell

Gustatory: sense of taste

It might be easiest for us to imagine visuals during mental rehearsal, but never underestimate the power of the other four senses, as well as emotional sensations. They're responsible for some of our strongest memories: the sound of a band, the smell of a rainy afternoon, the taste of an ice cream sundae, or the touch of a fuzzy sweater. During visualization, try as hard as you can to incorporate those other senses as well as how your scene looks to the eye.

Studies have shown that our brain chemistry treats imagined memories— visualization, that is—the same way as it treats *actual* memories. If you can visualize to a deep level, using all five senses and emotional projections, your brain is going to instill it as something you've already experienced. When you visualize jet-skiing, playing professional football, or being shot out of a cannon, your brain is just going to assume you've actually done so. You might logically know better, but emotionally you will be more even-keeled and calm, ready to tackle adversity.

This can be key in building your toughness. When you're about to do something you've never done before, most of the anxiety and tension you feel happens *before* you actually start doing it. The nervousness you feel in a new endeavor usually comes up when you're anticipating doing it. When you're actually doing it, most of that anxiety goes away.

Therefore, if the brain treats visualization the same way it treats real memories, you can "trick" your brain into building a belief in your own toughness. Sure, you might only be *visualizing* sky-diving, but if you do it thoroughly enough, your brain's going to think it really happened: "Ah, come on. We've sky-dived before. Remember? It's a piece of cake."

Believe it or not, this quirk of brain chemistry can boost your tenacity.

Schedule Every Hour

Toughness is tough. It requires the ability to regulate our time, stick to goals, and balance personal and family responsibilities. Toughness is even tougher when you have the freedom and time to veer off the correct path. It would be easier if someone like a drill sergeant was just forcing you into compliance. That's why scheduling can be so important: it lets you build a mentally tough approach to life, hour by hour and day by day.

When it comes to building toughness, it's not those one-off schedule disruptions that can stand in our way so much as our own desires. If too much of our time is unplanned or disordered, we tend to make decisions based on how we feel at the moment. We do something that's going to indulge what we want as opposed to what we know is right. Relying on willpower to keep going when we want to give up is risky to say the least; you can help yourself by strictly scheduling.

Putting a schedule down in writing will crystallize your intentions to not give up and keep persevering. We typically have the best of intentions that don't translate into actions, but seeing them written in front of you will bring clarity to what you are trying to achieve. It keeps our goals and commitments in plain sight. In strictly scheduling, you will remove all rash decision-making from your life, leaving you with a framework that is made with objective clarity, focused on the correct (tough) decisions versus the easy decisions.

Many of us use schedules for working hours, along with occasional appointments or family commitments. We generally don't schedule sleep, eating or bathing because those events usually happen at or near the same time every day. But to really keep us on track, reinforce our obligations, and thrive in our drive to tenacity, the optimal approach is setting a weekly schedule that accounts for every single hour of the week.

That's 168 hours, Sunday to Saturday. When you plan a schedule with that hour-by-hour exactness, it provides a fantastic overview of where your time goes and how many areas need more or less attention during the week—including where you are falling short in toughness.

Every last thing is budgeted in a 168-hour calendar, including sleeping, eating, social or family responsibilities, and recreation or relaxation. The process is to build a base of necessary functions that must be met and work upward to give every part of your daily life its proper allotment of your time and attention.

Basic needs. As strange as it might sound, all of your primary life functions should be entered on the 168-hour calendar. That includes sleeping, eating meals, bathing, and other matters of self-maintenance. In fact, these are the elements that the rest of the schedule is built around.

Adults generally sleep for about seven to eight hours a night. Personally, I'm something of a night owl, so my sleep schedule normally runs from 1:00 a.m. to 8:00 a.m. Since that single "activity" takes up the most disproportionately large part of the week, that goes in first. Next up are daily meals, including dinner preparation or travel time to restaurants. (By the way, a side benefit of scheduling meal times is that it could help you control your eating—but that's another book.) Following that are personal grooming, maintenance, and housekeeping items. These are all foundational needs that can determine how much willpower you have in each moment.

Occupational needs. Next, schedule your work-related activities. Even if you're unemployed, there's some daily work you do for reasons other than maintenance or recreation—whether it's writing, sewing, researching, craft-making, or some other pursuit. For those who are employed, it's great to get as specific as you possibly can for what you're going to do during the hours of the week: certain projects, office work, meetings, phone calls, responding to emails, or whatever else happens during a typical workday.

Some may choose to put housework and family responsibilities under "occupational needs," as they're something one has to do that doesn't necessarily reflect basic life functions. That's fine—it depends on your personal opinion. Personally, I see those as basic life functions, so I put them there. Your call.

Toughness. With all your basic and work needs meted out, the next step is to schedule in all of your tough but correct choices, as opposed to the easy path. This is where you schedule in everything that you'd rather not do but you know you should. Schedule it above pleasure, play, and anything else that would serve as a distraction.

This might consist of cooking healthy meals, going to the gym, or working on learning a new language. You might be reading more here or speaking with a counselor or therapist. You might be reading more of my critically acclaimed books. Whatever it is, you are making room for it in your life, prioritizing it above everything else besides work, family, sleep, and food. Toughness truly begins with daily actions that translate into habits. You can also schedule time to motivate yourself and remind yourself of the reasons to stay strong.

This will help you avoid moments of mental weakness, if you can just look at your schedule and understand what the correct choice should be.

At some point, you will hit the limits of your tenacity, and you'll have to take a breather. You're not trying to become a 24-hour machine of toughness and fortitude—at least not at first. You *will* need a break. You've scheduled time for sleep in your 168-hour schedule, after all.

You will need to relax at some point and restore yourself. Toughness isn't an infinite resource; it benefits from the act of recharging your batteries just as your attention and physical health do. In this scenario, your distractions are more than welcome to come back into your life—in fact, they could be incredibly helpful at this time.

But keep this in mind: pursue leisure with as much dedication as you're developing tenacity. Either relax completely or not at all. Don't let the boundary between work and leisure blur. When you're being lazy, be

100% lazy. Embrace your laziness. Slack off with total commitment.

Doing this will ultimately help you work better, because you're giving yourself enough downtime to build up your energy reserves. Don't work a lick during this part. Similarly, when you're totally devoted to working and not dropping off, it'll help you enjoy your moments of repose much more.

If you're going to lay on a pool float for a few hours, then give it your all, as long as you'll be able to pry yourself up from the couch and get back to work eventually.

When keeping to the schedule, pay close attention to these aspects of activity to make sure you're maximizing your calendar days.

Awareness. The number-one enemy of toughness is rationalization. It's especially insidious because it can happen on a subconscious level without too much in the way of conscious input. You might justify not sticking to the schedule because you think you can always make up for it at another time. Don't let this happen—the point of having a schedule is to stick to it until the task is complete or time is up.

Action. In addition to your schedule, you'd be best served by tracking the progress that you make in a certain effort. This is to make sure that the efforts you're making are having tangible results and to adjust your level of effort if you need to.

Attitude. Keeping your schedule current will give you a roadmap to getting where you need to go. It should give you a lot of confidence that you'll be able to accomplish what you set out to do if you follow the program. If you're confident you can do that, you've already conquered a major obstacle—so keep it in mind when you feel let down or tired.

Plan for Failure

At some point in your drive toward toughness, it's an inevitability that you will falter.

Both you and I want to believe you have the residual forces to sail through this effort and develop mental toughness without one moment of let-down or failure. But you won't. And that is not a terrible thing. It's just reality.

Any strategy for building toughness—or any strategy at all—needs to have a plan for failure: those moments when you fall totally out of line with your overall goal that would completely derail less disciplined or focused minds.

An important distinction is necessary here: I'm not talking about a "backup plan" or "plan B," which are alternate plans to obtain what you want in case one plan doesn't work out and which usually become the default for mental weakness. I'm talking about a plan for when the actions you've taken go completely against your goals— how you recover from total lapses, take a few steps retrograde, and then have to claw your way back to commitment.

Without such a plan in place, you may succumb to something called the "what-the-hell" effect. This is when you think you've blown enough already that you might as well forsake your goals and go headlong into regression.

Here's an example. Let's say you've set up a plan to be more physically active—at least three hours every day. With a full work or school load and time taken to eat and take basic care of yourself, that doesn't leave a lot of time. But you've managed to carve out enough. For a week, you pull it off. You feel change happening and it's going pretty well.

Then, one Friday night during your hour-long relaxation period, you get onto a streaming video site and see a new multi-episode show that everyone's been talking about. You take in the first episode and you're hooked, so you decide to watch the second immediately after. Then you take in the third episode. At some point you manage to go to sleep, but the next afternoon you find yourself desperately wanting to know what happens in the fourth episode. So you turn it on.

Three episodes later, you're in full-on binge mode, and you've decided to finish the series all in one sitting. You've already passed up the chance to get your three hours of physical exercise in by loafing on the couch for nine straight hours, so you know, *what the hell*? Go for the gusto and watch the whole thing. If it's just one season, well, that's one thing. But if it's a seven-season show like *Game of Thrones*, you might be in some trouble.

Faltering and slipping will happen. But throwing everything into a flaming garbage can is not a necessary part of the equation.

That's why you need to have a strategy in place to compensate for this eventuality and to work within your own realistic limits. If you know you're bound to fail more often than you like, instead of beating yourself up over your shortcomings, work them into your plan. For example, in the above war between better health and *Game of Thrones*, your recovery plan might be to swear off television for a few days after the binge and increase your physical activity period by a half-hour over those days. When the weekend comes and you have more time, you can schedule in two hours over each day of the weekend while going back to your three-hour physical activity rate during that time.

Think of your toughness in a scale of percentage. If you completely slip up and wake up in a location you don't remember traveling to, then that's 0% toughness. On the other hand, if you do absolutely nothing *but* work toward tenacity, that's 100% toughness. (And in that case, you might want to think about whether you're working a little too much.)

If you know you cannot personally sustain the level of toughness that you ultimately want to have—that's fine. Schedule a cushion to compensate. Instead of shooting for 100% toughness, you shoot for 90% toughness with 10% wiggle room. That 10% should be arranged so that you let out enough stress and pressure that you can reconvene quickly and go back to work. This means that when you slip up, only allow yourself to do it 10% of the way.

Accept that you will occasionally fail but try to limit your losses by setting a limit to your indulgence.

Sometimes the matter of getting back in line with your drive to toughness may be a little trickier. More failures have piled up, certain life events may have derailed your attention, and you're back to where you started.

But don't panic or throw all your plans out the window. If you feel you've gone too far in reverse or that getting back on the road to toughness is impossible, be assured there is a way back that involves making the most of square one. This is how you get back on track.

Identify the roots of your failure. Most likely you didn't stray off course because you "didn't want it badly enough." Sometimes outside factors intervene or changes have more of an effect than we bargained for. Take a careful accounting of everything that's happened while you've been sliding off the wagon and objectively consider whether it may have had an effect.

For example, you might have been trying to eat more healthy foods and avoid unhealthy ones, and you'd had a nice head start. But midway through your program you inherited a lot more responsibility at work, and it commanded all of your time and attention. It also created a whole new source of stress, no doubt. The new role didn't *make* you fall off your diet, but it took a lot of mental resources you needed to maintain it. You might have overeaten to deal with the new stress.

In this stage, you don't necessarily want to make a plan for what to do yet—you just want to know the root cause of why your lifestyle change program went astray. You just want a diagnosis. You don't need a cure yet.

Get back to the basics. Developing toughness is like any lifestyle change: it involves a lot of ambition, even if we don't think it's a big deal. You may have a sense of failure because you tried to do too much too quickly. Remember that any course of action that stretches you too far outside your current capacity is probably going to be ineffectual anyway. So when you're back at the bottom, reframe your efforts—scale back from the big ambition and just go back to basics. Make up some smaller goals that you can achieve more easily and build from them.

For example, you may have started a workout program with the goal of losing 40 pounds over the course of eight months. But you find yourself overexerting at the front of the program, trying to weight-train and overexercise to meet that goal as soon as you can. Scale it down: set smaller-gradient goals, like spending 30 minutes on a treadmill or going through circuit-training once every time you hit the gym. After you've made progress, you can increase your goals accordingly, but start from a smaller and more manageable set of objectives.

Embrace imperfect starts. A frequent source of frustration in building tenacity is when plans go awry. We can't put in as much time on the treadmill as we wanted because we get too tired too quickly. We can't start writing because we don't feel 100% comfortable in our creative environment. We want to start cooking for ourselves instead of going out, but we don't have a food processor.

We want everything to be in perfect condition for liftoff. But that perfect condition will almost never manifest. And there's *always* more than one way to achieve your goals. So if you stumble out of the gate or can't attain a perfect-world scenario to start changing, just embrace what you *do* have, adjust your goals, and just get underway. The point is to get started however you can, whether it's just a bit at a time or using alternate approaches to fit your situation.

Going back to our first-paragraph examples, if your limitations on the treadmill are causing you to doubt your ability to go through with the rest of the program, just do what you can and look for other ways to exercise in the meantime. If you're unable to write in your current environment, plug away on what you can while you look for other situations that might work. If you don't have a food processor for cooking at home, learn basic knife skills—there's a YouTube video for that.

Keep yourself accountable. A big reason we get off track in our ambitions is because we don't really have an effective means of checks and balances or an effective way to track our progress. Many times, we start life-changing programs in a sort of vacuum, because we're trying to do things we haven't done before. Since we don't have that experience, sometimes we aren't sure how to measure what we're doing.

There are a few ways to keep yourself accountable when you're trying to get back up. One way is to consult with somebody who knows us well, knows what we're trying to accomplish, and can give you objective input on how you're doing and the changes they see happening. This is especially effective when somebody who's actually *counting* on you to change—a family member, a work associate, or a close friend—can help out.

Alternately, you can set up a system of self-tracking yourself. A great way to do this is through journaling or record-keeping: writing down what you do toward your goal every day or tracking growth or change through a spreadsheet. This system is extremely under-used considering how solid data-driven solutions can be and how effective it is.

Probably the most obvious example for keeping yourself accountable is physical fitness—you can keep track of how many miles you walk or spend on a treadmill, how many circuits you finish (and how you increase your strength over time), or your daily calorie intake. But if you're trying to develop a more tenacious character at work or in social settings, you can keep track of your personal reflections about your interactions throughout the day in a written journal.

Try a different approach. There comes a point where, if you've tried the same strategy time after time with little or no success, it might be time to try something different. If the low-carb diet doesn't seem to be helping, try a vegetarian one. If you're stumbling trying to write fiction, try writing nonfiction or personal reflections for a while. If you're not having a lot of success weightlifting, try Nautilus circuit-training for a bit.

Repeatedly forcing yourself to try and fit into a program that just doesn't help won't work—there's no magic number of times you can keep trying it until it all finally comes together. So don't be afraid to start from scratch with an entirely new approach. It might raise awareness of areas that the old approach simply wasn't addressing effectively.

Finally, be kind to yourself. Toughness does not grow in a vacuum, and it does not grow in accordance with low self-esteem. Grant yourself the leeway to fail and fail hard. Understand that this is human and that it's all part of a process that leads to improvement but not necessarily perfection.

Dealing with Distractions

Finally, the road to toughness is replete with obstacles, but none may be as sneaky as the distractions that come up. We could be humming along, building our resources up in a consistent and sturdy fashion, when out of nowhere comes a phone call, a breaking news bulletin on TV, or those most diabolical attention-yankers of all: kitten videos.

Distractions lure us back into a state of complacency and inertia. Our inner pleasure-seeker goes through distractions like paper napkins. They're the cause of delay, inattention, and even outright cancellation of our most well-laid plans. How should we deal with them?

For this, we have to look at the example of Spanish conquistador Hernán Cortés in 1519. Cortés sailed what's now the Gulf of Mexico with his army on ships, and they landed on the shores of the Aztec Empire with designs on conquering it. Cortés was concerned that some of his men would take the chicken exit, remove themselves from his ranks, go back to the ships, and sail to Cuba, where things were relatively quiet.

Cortés's solution? Burn the ships.

These were not cheap ships. They cost a lot to make. They had taken Cortés's entire fleet across the Atlantic Ocean and housed all their necessary supplies. And now Cortés was saying to burn them all down? Yes, he was.

Cortés didn't want his men to have any chance of leaving the mission. He wanted to remove any possible avenues of escape, even if it meant losing some of the most expensive sea vessels in the world. He wanted to rid his ranks of all cowards and force them to go on with their mission and not give them any opportunity to retreat. So get out the flame lanterns and oily rags, he commanded.

I'm not suggesting you set fire to everything that may cause distraction in your drive to tenacity. But you *can* take inventory of potential distractions that could temporarily pull you from your responsibilities. Remember that willpower is not your trustworthy friend when dealing with the lures of the pleasure principle, so you're going to have to force yourself to make it work. It's truly best when you don't even have to rely on it and just do it as a result of your environment.

Here's what you do. Make a list of all the things that draw your attention away from important things—TV, smartphone, tablet, laptop, videos, music, whatever you got.

Then make it extremely difficult to pay attention to those distractions while you're working on your tenacity. Unplug your TV and speakers. Take the battery out of your smartphone and other devices (if you can—if not, turn it off and store it somewhere out of sight). Pull the curtains down on your windows if they're overlooking a street. If you need your laptop to work on, disable the browsers and make it difficult to bring them back.

Some people will find that course of action drastic and unbearable—and that's the point. With those distractions out of the way, you're going to have to be more resourceful and creative and push yourself to get things finished. Guess what that does? That's right: *builds toughness.*

Takeaways:

- Even though mental toughness can be said to be an exercise in willpower, it can benefit from structure and strategy.

- The first strategy to create more toughness is to use visualization. Visualization assists with building toughness because it takes you through fearful steps and lets you know that you will be okay.

- Second, use a strict, detailed daily schedule. After scheduling in your basic human needs, schedule in time for toughness. Put your best intentions onto the schedule so you can stare at them daily. Prioritize this time over everything else.

- Plan for failure. No one is perfect, and we will all falter from time to time in our quest for toughness. But we can set a limit to our indulgence. This is distinct from a backup plan because a plan for failure is about how to recover and limit losses, whereas a backup plan is about an alternate course of action.

- Distractions? Burn them, I say. Make them impossible to access and make it so your willpower doesn't need to be used.

Chapter 4. Win the Battle Against Yourself

If you're going through hell, keep going. – Winston Churchill

Mike always wanted to be a journalist. He got into television news at an unusually young age and was up on current events even in elementary school. Journalism sounded like a great way to see the world and experience different cultures, so he majored in journalism and interned at a news outlet during his senior year of college.

But Mike was dismayed at the station. A couple of people were interested in him and took him under their wings, but there were plenty of others who were gruff and more concerned with their own work than his own development. Even the people who apparently liked him had to leave to do their own things.

Mike considered this his own fault. He wasn't pushy enough, he thought. He didn't think his insights into current events were anything special in this cut-throat environment. He took other people's indifference as proof that he wasn't special. It made him anxious and fearful.

Then Mike had a few too many to drink one night when he was alone in his apartment and terribly disconsolate. His whole pursuit was ridiculous, he thought. TV journalists are always flawless-looking and attractive, whereas he had a birthmark on his neck that he was sure disqualified him from on-camera work. Even if his stories were well-researched and thought-provoking, there was no use in fighting for them in the "war room" because they weren't "sensational" or "sexy" enough. The entire operation was aligned against people like Mike.

The next day, Mike abruptly quit, gave notice at his apartment, and was never seen by the TV station or any of his associates again. Word has it that he works at a maritime insurance company looking for damage fraud. It's a complete waste of his talents, but that's how things go when the universe is always against you.

Mike works, goes home, has a modest dinner, goes to sleep, and does the whole thing over again the next day. On Wednesdays, though, he watches his favorite reality TV show: *Real Housewives of Someday Isle*. Goodness, they always seem so miserable.

This chapter is about how we get in our own way with negative thoughts and doomsday scenarios. Mike was unable to break through his fixation on failure and grounded himself before ever getting started. Winning the battle against yourself is the most important step to toughness. We're going to examine some ways to coach the mind into changing those deep-seated beliefs to give us the clarity and fortitude to stick with it and build tenacity.

Battle Your Beliefs

With all we've talked about regarding toughness, it might surprise you that one of the principles we turn to now is the power of belief. But that's because, beneath everything, if you simply don't believe in yourself, none of the rest matters. To get anywhere, you must believe that you can.

To illustrate, we turn to Sir Roger Bannister. The name Roger Bannister may not be familiar to you unless you're a track and field fan or a historian of athletics.

In 1954, Roger Bannister was the first man to break the four-minute barrier for the mile, which was a long-standing threshold that people had flirted with constantly but had never crossed.

One complete mile is four laps around a standard track. This means to break the four-minute threshold, a runner would need a pace of, at most, 60 seconds per lap—something that was thought to be impossible. The whole idea that a human being could run a mile in under four minutes was thought to be fantasy, and even track experts predicted that humans would never do it. You have to remember that this was years ago when competitive athletics were still in their nascent stage—nothing close to the training, nutrition, or attention we can use today. These athletes were competing on methods that are absolutely prehistoric in comparison to modern techniques.

The world record for the mile was stalled around 4:02 and 4:01 for over a decade, so there seemed to be some truth to the belief that humans had finally reached their physical potential. It had been lowered steadily up to that point, starting from the first modern Olympics in 1896—the gold medalist of the 1,500 meters won in a time of 4:33, which is the rough equivalent of a 4:46 mile. We had come so far, there had to be a limit, and we seemed to have hit it. Of course, similar notions of limits of human capabilities have existed in more modern times, such as the 10-second barrier for the 100-meter dash. For comparison's sake, the world record for the mile at of the end of

2018 is 3:43.13, held by Hicham El Guerrouj of Morocco.

At the 1952 Helsinki Summer Olympics, Bannister finished in fourth place in the 1,500-meter run (the *metric* mile), just short of receiving a medal. Motivated by his disappointment and shame, he set his sights on running a sub-four-minute mile, which he felt would exonerate him. Bannister, unlike all other runners and experts at the time, believed that it was possible, so he trained with that in mind. It was a matter of *when*, not *if*, for him. Just making the assumption that something is a certainty, and even planning for what happens when you surpass it, can force you to behave in a drastically different manner.

All the while a doctor-in-training, Bannister began in earnest to attempt breaking the threshold in 1954. He accomplished the feat on May 6 by 0.6 seconds in a time of 3:59.4. People were in disbelief, and he was revered as superhuman. For his efforts, he was knighted in 1975 and enjoyed a long life representing British athletic interests both domestically and internationally. Again, he accomplished this all while he was a practicing doctor and neurologist.

Here's where belief truly comes into the story of Sir Roger Bannister and the four-minute mile. Within two months of his breaking the four-minute mark, an Australian runner named John Landy broke both the four-minute mark *and* Bannister's world record. The following year, three other runners also broke the four-minute mark. The next decade saw over a dozen people break the four-minute mark that had stymied runners for years.

Such is the power of belief. People have preconceptions about what is possible and what is out of their reach. But most of the time, that simply limits them. They allow themselves to be disenfranchised by what they perceive to be possible or not, what they perceive they are capable of or not, and what they can be.

When you believe, that's a beautiful thing that can take us to great heights, including toughness. Belief is something that is self-perpetuating. When you have it, you create more of it because it drives you to triumph after triumph.

Without it, you are putting an arbitrary limit on yourself. You sabotage yourself and may never even get started.

In the months following Bannister's achievement, nothing about those other four runners changed physically. They didn't magically grow winged feet or use performance-enhancing drugs as today's athletes might. They didn't alter their training habits or regimens. All that conceivably could have changed was their mindset of belief—they were certain the four-minute threshold could be beaten, and they were going to do it! That was the only element that changed.

Roger Bannister redefined what was possible and instilled others with belief. If Bannister had lacked belief that his goal was achievable, he would have been happy with a time of 4:01 and in regret for the rest of his life when someone else like John Landy came along and was first to break the tape in under four minutes. Your lack of belief is often your biggest obstacle to toughness. What level of toughness are you settling for, because you lack the belief that you can be more?

Believe that you can persevere in the face of fear. Believe that you won't give up of your own free will. Believe that you are someone who will keep walking when they are in hell. And you will become that person.

Battle Your Self-Talk

Negativity in the form of our inner voice is hard to shake since it tends to overwhelm the positive. Pessimism is usually easier to articulate than optimism, especially with those who aren't organized to see the good in most situations. Complaining is easier than complimenting, and telling yourself you can't achieve something is easier than declaring that you can.

To battle that despairing outlook, it's necessary to alter your relationship with yourself. There are a few ways to speak to yourself to make you feel more empowered and tough.

A first step is to remind yourself who holds the key to your own fate. You guessed it: you. You can never stand on the sidelines when it comes to what you do. Even when "things happen to you," you're in charge of your reaction to those events and your next steps. The responsibility of turning those disadvantages into change falls on your shoulders. You don't have an outside supervisor to answer to—you're in control.

So the best path to take is to be proactive. Understand that when it comes to yourself, you're the only one in charge. Accepting that fact should free you up to form your own reality—the one that *you're* after. Nobody else has such complete access or vision into your ambitions or dreams. You're pretty much the only one that can most reliably help yourself build the world you want to live in.

That should be a *freeing* idea to you. It means you can do this using only your own ideas and desires. Outside resources are, again, "nice-to-haves." But they're not "*necessary*-to-haves." You already have all that's necessary. You have total control.

Then there's the question of luck. We're all subject to gains and losses due to circumstances we have no way of managing. But is luck really the deciding factor in the stories of our lives?

A lot of people think so. They believe that luck is a huge factor in what makes some people succeed and other people fail. This notion is disempowering—it connotes that you can't do anything about your own success. But it's also seductive in that it absolves us of responsibility for our failures, like those excuses we talked about a couple of chapters ago.

What do successful people think about luck? Most of them acknowledge that they've had some lucky breaks, that certain events outside their command may have influenced their prosperity. But they don't *rely* on luck at all, because they can't. It's not something they can manage anyway, so they move forward with what they can do.

For the same reason of undermining the power of luck, they don't worry about bad luck happening to them—it's a negative prospect that would only detract from what they need to do. If they gave that much energy to anxiety about bad luck, they'd have little left over to build on what they have.

So don't get consumed by the possibility of terrible luck and what might happen to you—it's a useless expense of your finite mental faculties. Instead, make positive efforts to build your world the way you want to have it and make good things happen. You can't stop outside bad luck from happening, but you can manage what *you* do to change your situation.

Your mind is always having an inner dialogue with itself. Whether or not you actually verbalize these exchanges, it's constantly running through the entire course of your day. It's how you process the decisions you make and the actions you take. It's usually a push and pull between positive and negative aspects—and frequently it's the negative side that's coming through in louder volume.

Negative self-talk isn't always directly disempowering—it's not just saying, "I can't do this" or "I'm unable to do this." It can also be subtly disguised as goal-stating: "I *should* do this." That's saying there's an action you *can* do at the present time but still *aren't*. That leaves an opening for some other kind of statement to take over and get you off-track.

You can counteract negative self-talk by consciously structuring your internal statements to be more constructive and motivational. To battle that negative, self-defeating inner voice, your self-talk should be structured in three ways.

Positive. Obviously, positive is how you neutralize negative. Your self-talk needs to contain affirmative statements. "I am working hard on my science project, it is getting better every day, and it will end up exactly as I want." This is ground zero for empowering self-talk. It might feel a bit like you are appealing to the law of attraction or affirmations, but the truth is, *they* are the derivatives of self-talk. "I'm going to be tough in this situation. I've done it before and it will be easy."

Specific. Self-talk that's too general allows for anything to happen. The more exact you can be with your statements and aspirations, the more powerful your self-messaging will be. Rather than say, "I'm going to get better at work," say, "I'm improving my interactions with workmates and showing up on time." This gives you an exact guideline to follow and makes you focus on what you need to do. "I'm going to be tougher in this situation by making sure to react logically, think about the positive aspects, and realize that the long-term negatives are nonexistent."

Present tense. Your self-talk has to reflect what is happening now—it will suggest that you're actively working instead of procrastinating until the future. So instead of saying, "I should get started on that workout regimen," say, "I am working out."

This is a subtle change in language that makes it clear that things are happening now and are tangible instead of still being aspirational or ethereal. "I am tough. I am resilient. This is easy." Using the present tense gives you no wiggle room—this is happening right now, and you are achieving it.

Like the visualizations from the last chapter, your subconscious processes positive self-talk as accurate, even if you haven't yet done what you're telling it you've done. By speaking them out, your brain is dealing with them as if they're already reality. The more positive your messages become, the stronger and more tenacious you become.

Negativity Bias and Coping with Failure

Why do cutting remarks made years ago still stick in the craw? Why are so many political campaign ads so relentlessly negative? Why do we watch news reports about scandals and disasters with great attention but don't register as much interest in stories about people doing good in their communities?

Simply put, our brains are biased in favor of negativity. Bad events, tragedies, insults, and calamity have more of an impact on our brains than positive events. This has actually been borne out by scientific research: an Ohio State University study showed that the brain's cerebral cortex experiences a higher level of electrical activity when exposed to negative stimuli than positive. Our stronger reactions to negative events are simply a matter of biology.

In a way, negativity bias is a defense mechanism—the brain is more attuned to recognizing and calling out threats so we can put our survival instincts to work and flee the situation. But it also overrides positive messaging to a greater degree, so it's even more important to focus on positive self-talk and treating ourselves with more kindness in situations where we've fallen short or experienced disappointment.

Taking failure personally is understandable and common. It's extremely hard for us to be consoled when we've gone through a tremendous letdown—and it might even be harder to forgive ourselves and move forward. Your self-talk in the aftermath of failure therefore needs to be especially positive.

It's okay. You'll be okay. The first line of defense against negativity in failure is simply "this too shall pass." Personal failures never spell the end of your story or your life. There may be a few bumps in the emotional road in the very near future, but you'll emerge on the other side of it and be ready to move forward again soon.

There is no success without failure. The total number of success stories that have come into being without a single moment of failure is exactly zero. Every single person that's experienced great moments of triumph has experienced at least one or two flops and likely more. Without the requisite background in failure from which to learn how to adjust and improve, they wouldn't have experienced true success. People who *don't* make mistakes probably don't have the audacity to take risks, so they rarely produce anything of value. It's far worse to not try something and live with regret about it than to take a big shot and fall flat.

Success is always closer than it seems. Mistakes inform us what to do and change to succeed. Therefore, if we pivot from our mistakes, avoid excuses, and use what we've learned to adjust, failure can be a strong motivator for the future. With that in mind, the turnaround from loss to win can occur much more quickly than it might seem during moments of letdown. As the saying goes, "Failure is not falling down— it's staying down." In that context, the only mistake we can really make is not doing anything. The sooner we get back to work, the stronger our chance of success.

You are not your mistakes. You can't allow your defeats to define who you are. Yes, it's difficult *not* to take failure personally, especially if we've devoted so many of our resources in the name of winning. Again, the biggest success stories of our time contain subplots that depict utter failure—

but the characters in those stories refused to wear that failure on their sleeves. So should you. Accept that mistakes are inevitable, if not always foreseeable, and resolve to move on. With that thinking, your entire future is a blank slate waiting for you to draw some success on it.

Life goes on. Years down the line, your shortfalls, errors, and failures will just be part of a long backstory. With that distance between now and then, your failures will be much easier to deal with. You might even be in the position to look back on them and laugh, as a lot of people project when they're trying to dig themselves out of a hole. Always be willing to learn from your mistakes rather than succumb to the destructive force of regret.

Nothing that's worthwhile comes easy. Instant gratification is the order of the day. We can get what we want more quickly than ever. We look at our role models for success and think they make it look so easy. But if success really *were* a walk in the park, then everybody on earth would be walking around in pure bliss. I have it on good authority they're not. Just remember that taking a high risk is the only way to receive a high reward—and sometimes those risks will fall short. But don't back down. When you want something badly enough, you'll have to withstand multiple moments of failure. If you learn from them, you're opening the door for improvement and making the chance of great things happening that much more likely.

Battle Your Supposed Limits

Maximizing human toughness in the way that Navy SEALs push themselves to do has led to the development of a famous rule known as the 40% rule.

The 40% rule is straightforward. It says that when an individual's mind begins telling them that they are physically or emotionally maxed out, in reality they have only pushed themselves to 40% of their full capacity. In other words, they could endure 60% more if only they believed that they are capable of it. When you think you have reached your limits, you're not even close, and whether you can keep going or not depends on if you believe it. It's quite a belief to feel that you've reached your limits and say to yourself that you're only 40% done. It's an acceptance of pain and a message you send clearly to yourself. *You can do more. In fact, you haven't even started yet.*

We are usually ready to give up around the time that we begin to feel pain or are barely pressing our boundaries. But that point is actually just the beginning of what we are all capable of, and the key to unlocking more potential is to push through the initial pain and the self-doubt that surfaces along with it. By maintaining a belief in yourself, you show yourself that you can do more, and that evidence builds your confidence and mental toughness.

You might, for example, begin struggling after doing 10 push-ups. You'd start hearing the voice in your head that says you feel too tired, too sore, or too weak to go on. But if you take a pause and gather yourself to do one more, you find that you've already disproven the voice saying that you can't.

Then you pause and do another. And then another.

And then another. Suddenly you're at 20. You can take it slowly, but you've just doubled what you thought was possible.

Believing that you can do more will make it true. It enables you to go well beyond the limits that you've constructed for yourself in your own mind. And once you've felt the pain and the urge to give up at 10 push-ups only to push through it and do 20, you know that your mental strength helped you persevere. The next time you're challenged, you'll feel all the more capable and prepared to push past your supposed limits again. This embodies self-discipline in a nutshell—it's really a matter of how much pain you can stomach, and most of us will only bend and never break.

Our minds can be our best friends when we have a strong belief in our capabilities, but they can also be a poisonous enemy if we allow negativity to seize control. It's up to you to empower yourself using the 40%

rule rather than throwing in the towel mentally at the first sign of resistance.

Imagine that you decide to run a 5k or even a full marathon despite being out of shape. Inevitably, as you run, you'll begin to breathe harder, your legs will feel heavier, and you might question yourself. You could easily give up in that moment and save yourself from extra pain and soreness. But if circumstances were different and you were running away from danger out of self-preservation, you could undoubtedly continue on well beyond that first inclination to give in. Barring massive injuries, you'd finish if you believed the pain was part of the process. It's all a matter of whether you believe you can or not.

The reality is, most of us have no clue about our true physical and mental limitations. Our lives are so much safer and more comfortable than those of our ancestors, and that has some undesirable consequences when it comes to mental strength. We don't test ourselves and we don't know what we're capable of. Now it is mostly the people who seek out intense challenges that subsequently learn discipline and mental strength, while the rest go about their comfortable lives without any idea of their full capabilities.

In case you're skeptical as to the merits of the 40% rule, there is some scientific evidence in support of it that might help convince you. Numerous studies over the years have found that the placebo effect—the tangible change in performance caused merely by a belief that something you've done will impact performance—has a significant impact, especially in athletics. The legitimacy of the placebo effect suggests that your mental strength and toughness play a big role in physical abilities. In other words, if you believe it, it will *be*.

One powerful demonstration of the placebo effect comes from a 2008 study published in the *European Journal of Neuroscience.* The study found that giving participants sugar pills and telling them that it was caffeine made them work significantly harder when they subsequently lifted weights. The belief that they would have extra strength and energy allowed the participants to tap further into their own potential without even being aware of it.

There is a scientific consensus that the placebo effect is not a deception, fluke, experimental bias, or statistical anomaly. Rather, it is a self-fulfilling prophecy in which the human brain anticipates an outcome and then produces that outcome of its own accord. In fact, the placebo effect closely follows the types of patterns you would expect to see if the brain was really producing its own desired results. Researchers have illustrated this phenomenon by showing that placebos follow the same dose-response curves as real medicines. Two pills give more relief than one, a larger pill has a stronger effect than a smaller one, and so on.

When you consider the placebo effect, it quickly becomes clear how powerful our minds are. Countless studies have supported the conclusion that the placebo effect is a result of chemical changes in the form of endorphin production. Just believing that you can give 60% more effort makes it possible.

Apart from athletic performance studies, the classic examples of the placebo effect are medical studies where people are given dummy pills but experience similar effects as the participants who were given the actual medications or vitamins. An interesting case is when people are given placebo painkillers and actually report alleviated pain. That the placebo effect can even impact pain suggests that any process controlled by our brains can be "tricked" by having a positive expectation.

So the placebo effect can obviously be used for performance enhancement, but how can it be applied to self-discipline?

Imagine how your odds of overcoming a strong addiction might change based on your attitude about that addiction. Believing that it's going to be hard and that you might not be capable will make failure a lot more likely than if you expect that you'll overcome the addiction. That's not to say that you should be naive and take a challenge lightly, but rather that you'll likely get the result that you expect to get.

For any goals that you have, struggles with discipline can probably be overcome by changing your expectations. The 40% rule and the placebo effect both ultimately show that all of us are more capable than we give ourselves credit for. Whenever you find yourself making excuses or lacking discipline, consider those two phenomena and ask if your excuses are legitimate. Quite often, the underlying causes of lapses in discipline are the beliefs we create in our minds that we can't do something. Expecting yourself to be capable, successful, and disciplined will make it all the more likely that you actually are.

Battle Your Emotions

Expressing your emotions is vital to mental health and resiliency. But there is another step that mentally tough people take to ensure they make balanced, well-thought-through decisions—they aren't reactive to what happens on a daily level. To be successful in regulating your emotions, your ability to think long-term instead of focusing on the day-to-day nitty-gritty of life will prove invaluable.

Many people make the mistake of spending too much of their time focused on the immediate future or sucked into the status quo. Instead, you should consciously choose to zoom out and look at the broader picture in order to gain control over your emotions. Focusing on small setbacks that occur in the short-term can skew your view of what matters in the long-term.

Let's pretend that you had set a goal to eat more whole foods and produce on a daily basis.

On Friday, you didn't manage to eat a salad with your lunch, and on Sunday you went out with friends and ate an entire plate of deep-fried Buffalo wings. Many people may focus on the short-term and berate themselves for making such poor choices in relation to their goal. However, by choosing to zoom out and look at the broader picture, these two examples may be only tiny blips on the radar. You only have cause for concern when there are numerous blips and a pattern begins to form.

No, you didn't meet your goal on Friday and Sunday, but perhaps when looking at the entire month it will become clear that you have been making great strides toward eating more whole foods and produce on a daily basis. When looking at a single day, small deviations from your goal may loom large and seem like overwhelming setbacks. However, when viewing your choices for an entire month, the true impact of an occasional small daily setback will become clear. A small setback on the daily scale does not derail a long-term goal.

By simply adjusting your perspective, you are able to identify small setbacks, such as eating a plate of wings with your friends, and move on much more quickly and with less stress and negativity. In general, if an event will seem unimportant or forgettable in a few days, then it is not worth holding on to or dwelling on.

Choosing to focus on the immediate moment causes you to engage with life in a very reactive manner: you are emotional, prone to making quick, ill-thought-through decisions, and easily derailed by day-to-day setbacks. Instead of living in this reactive manner, those with mental toughness make a conscious choice to live their lives in a state of controlled deliberateness. They are logical, measured, and consider the long-term implications of their decision before setting a course of action. Everyone encounters day-to-day ups and downs, but obsessing over short-term wins or losses is a waste of energy.

Olympic athletes are a fantastic example of individuals who shrug off short-term wins or losses to remain fixated on their long-term goals. Whether an athlete encounters a minor injury, a first-place trophy in a national competition, or unexpected training challenges, the long-term goal does not change. These small occurrences hold little weight in the face of an Olympic medal two or three years in the future. Resilient, strong individuals know that you must focus on what you can control each day, put in the hard work to move toward your goals, and live your life in a controlled, deliberate manner.

To further contrast the difference between living your life in an emotional, reactionary manner and choosing to be controlled and deliberate, consider the following scenario:

> You have $86,400 in your checking account. While getting into your car one evening, a thief approaches and robs you. He manages to steal $10 from your wallet. Would you spend your remaining $86,390 hiring private investigators and lawyers to find and prosecute the thief? Or would you recognize that in the long-term $10 means very little to you and it is better to appreciate the events that have gone well in your life and move on from this small setback?

In this scenario, choosing to find and prosecute the thief would be an example of emotional and reactionary living. It may feel good in the short-term to give in to your emotions, especially because this event might seem huge when zoomed into your timeline of the day, but it ultimately squanders your time and can negatively impact your ability to attain your long-term goals. Instead, those with mental resiliency and strength choose to think long-term.

They zoom out on their timeline and take into account what $10, a small amount of money, truly means when considering the full amount they have in their checking account. They understand that it is a waste to spend the remaining $86,390 and instead choose to move on from this short-term setback and continue making progress toward their goals.

Some of you may have made the connection that there are 86,400 seconds in one day. This scenario can also be viewed in the context of a single day. Should you waste an entire day focusing on one 10-second setback? Of course not! That would be just as wasteful as squandering $86,390. When thinking about this 10 seconds or $10 in the future, it will seem inconsequential. A small setback, when you zoom out on your timeline, becomes recognizable for what it is—insignificant.

Humans are evolutionarily hardwired to react emotionally. Emotions are immediate and reactionary. To live in a controlled and deliberate manner requires logic. Due to our evolutionary hardwiring, it can take time for logical thought to be restored after an emotional setback. It is physically impossible for reactive emotions and logical thought to be occurring simultaneously within our brains.

Therefore, mentally tough individuals choose to take some time before reacting to setbacks. This allows their brains time to process the emotional reaction and move back into logical thought before making any decisions or taking action. Never react immediately. Always allow yourself time to calm down and clearly think through decisions or actions before committing yourself.

To master these skills, zoom out and look at the broader picture. Day-to-day wins or setbacks are inconsequential when viewed on a broader scale. Always choose to live your life with controlled deliberateness instead of allowing yourself to inhabit a short-term reactionary space. And ensure that after emotional setbacks, you allow yourself time to calm down and let your brain settle back into logical thought before committing to a course of action.

A final way to think long-term is to travel through time and think in terms of 10-10-10. The next time you feel you're about to lose your mental fortitude and give in, stop and try to transport yourself 10 minutes, 10 hours, and 10 days from the current moment. The idea is to disconnect from the emotional present by thinking about a time when you are calm and unaffected.

This may not seem so powerful, but it forces you to think specifically about your future self, specifically the future self that you are aspiring to. In the next 10 minutes, hours, and days, you want to view yourself as emotionally even and balanced. A lot of times, we may know that we are doing something harmful in the moment, but that's not enough to stop us from doing it because we don't have any connection to our future self that will have to deal with the consequences.

Someone has just cut you off in traffic and almost caused you to crash. There was no damage done, but you are livid and on the verge of chasing them down in your car and assaulting them. What if you were to think about your mental state in 10 minutes, hours, and days? Think about what you'll be doing, what you would be feeling if the event didn't occur, and where you would be.

In a sense, you are distracting yourself from the current emotional moment by reminding yourself that you have a life to live, and your current rage will keep you from doing that. Control your emotions by looking ahead to the rest of your life and visualizing how you want it to go.

There is an old Zen saying: "Your anger, depression, spite, or despair, so seemingly real and important right now; where will they have gone in a month, a week, or even a moment?"

Intense emotions blind us to the future and con us that now is all that matters. In fact, when we are incredibly angry or anxious, we can forget that there is even going to *be* a future. We've all said or done things we later regret simply because, for a time, we let ourselves be dictated by our own emotion. Look beyond the immediate and you'll see the bigger picture and calm down, too.

Takeaways:

- The biggest enemy you will face in your life is always going to be you. You are going to empower yourself or let yourself be a perpetual victim. The only difference is if you approach the world with a degree of toughness and perseverance.

- Toughness stems from mindset and thought. You need to first believe that you are capable of something before it is even remotely possible. For that, we turn to the story of Roger Bannister and how the power of belief led to his track and field records being repeatedly smashed.
- The narrative you tell yourself quite literally comes from how you speak to yourself. We call this self-talk. Again, it can be used to encourage and motivate you or simply bring you down. This is especially important because humans have a biological imperative to focus on the negative. Your self-talk should be uplifting, focused on the present tense, and specific to the point of being instructive.
- Feeling like you've hit your limit? You're wrong. That's an excuse, and we know excuses are lies. This message is brought to you by the 40% rule of pushing your threshold for pain and discomfort.

- Finally, your emotions are a large part of mental lapses. Sometimes, we mistake reality for what we feel. This is only human, but it makes you reactive to the world instead of maintaining control. The most immediate way to battle your haywire emotions is to zoom out and gain a long-term view of life, your hardships, and how ephemeral they all are. Over time, a setback is but a blip. Errors are reversible. Turmoil is forgotten. Toughness is for life.

Cheat Sheet

Chapter 1. Toughness Determines Your Life

- Toughness is simply one of the keys to life. It gets you wherever you want to go, and it accurately realizes that the biggest obstacle in life is yourself. If we aren't able to embody toughness and persevere through hardships, we will inevitably end up on Someday Isle. That is not a pleasant vacation spot; it's more of a purgatory where people go when they've given up. And it's tough to escape.
- Toughness is sabotaged by a few toxic patterns of thought. These include cynicism, negativism, defeatism, escapism, and delayism.
- Dopamine is one of the most important aspects of toughness. We lack toughness because we seek the instant gratification of dopamine. This causes us to give up, binge, relax, and otherwise make the

easy or pleasurable choice over the correct and tougher choice. We want dopamine too much and too frequently. We can battle this by using the placebo effect, using a positive spin, giving yourself deadlines, and breaking down tasks to create greater feelings of accomplishment.

- The toughness résumé is something for your eyes only. It's a reminder of just how tough you've been in your life, whether willingly or not. This will change the narrative of who you are as a person—what's on the résumé is who you are, and that's hard evidence! Use this to stay tough in difficult times when all you want to do is throw in the towel and give up. You've faced worse and lived, so you can face the current day as well.

Chapter 2. Your Excuses Are Lies

- Let's get this out of the way up front: excuses are lies. Excuses are the very epitome of giving up in the face of adversity, because excuses create a reality where adversity doesn't exist. They are the easy way out and lead you down a path of learned helplessness and playing the victim.

- Even worse, excuses lead to self-handicapping, which is otherwise known as "I can't fail if I don't try." Not only is that detrimental to toughness, but it also drags down your entire outlook to life.

- Some excuses are real, and we distinguish them by calling them reasons. Reasons are focused on your personal responsibility and agency in a matter. Reasons epitomize toughness because they recognize a hardship and choose to look at it straight on and persevere.

- Common excuse patterns include playing the perfectionist, blaming the environment, being too intimidated, and being a defeatist. A method to defeat these excuse patterns, as well as any other excuses in general, is to look for three components of your situation: the truth, the mentally weak conclusion, and the mentally strong conclusion. Finding the separation between these perspectives is how you can realize which path you should take.

Chapter 3. Strategize Against Apathy, Weakness, and Giving Up

- Even though mental toughness can be said to be an exercise in willpower, it can benefit from structure and strategy.

- The first strategy to create more toughness is to use visualization. Visualization assists with building toughness because it takes you through fearful steps and lets you know that you will be okay.

- Second, use a strict, detailed daily schedule. After scheduling in your basic human needs, schedule in time for toughness. Put your best intentions onto the schedule so you can stare at them daily. Prioritize this time over everything else.

- Plan for failure. No one is perfect, and we will all falter from time to time in our quest for toughness. But we can set a limit to our indulgence. This is distinct from a backup plan because a plan for failure is about how to recover and limit losses, whereas a backup plan is about an alternate course of action.

- Distractions? Burn them, I say. Make them impossible to access and make it so your willpower doesn't need to be used.

Chapter 4. Win the Battle Against Yourself

- The biggest enemy you will face in your life is always going to be you. You are going to empower yourself or let yourself be a perpetual victim. The only difference is if you approach the world with a degree of toughness and perseverance.
- Toughness stems from mindset and thought. You need to first believe that you are capable of something before it is even remotely possible. For that, we turn to the story of Roger Bannister and how the power of belief led to his track

159

and field records being repeatedly
smashed.

- The narrative you tell yourself quite
  literally comes from how you speak to
  yourself. We call this self-talk. Again, it
  can be used to encourage and motivate
  you or simply bring you down. This is
  especially important because humans
  have a biological imperative to focus on
  the negative. Your self-talk should be
  uplifting, focused on the present tense,
  and specific to the point of being
  instructive.

- Feeling like you've hit your limit? You're
  wrong. That's an excuse, and we know
  excuses are lies. This message is brought
  to you by the 40% rule of pushing your
  threshold for pain and discomfort.

- Finally, your emotions are a large part of
  mental lapses. Sometimes, we mistake
  reality for what we feel. This is only
  human, but it makes you reactive to the
  world instead of maintaining control.
  The most immediate way to battle your
  haywire emotions is to zoom out and
  gain a long-term view of life, your
  hardships, and how ephemeral they all

are. Over time, a setback is but a blip.
Errors are reversible. Turmoil is
forgotten. Toughness is for life.

69875571R00097